Memories of Breaston, Draycott, Long Eaton and Sawley

Reminiscences from local folk collected by Julia Powell

© Copyright 2019 Julia Powell

All rights reserved.
No part of this publication may be reproduced, stored in a retrieval system, or transmitted, in any form or by any means, electronic, mechanical, photocopying, recording or otherwise, without the prior written permission of the editor.

British Library Cataloguing in Publication Data.
A catalogue record for this book is available
from the British Library

ISBN 978 0 86071 785 0

A Commissioned Publication Printed by
MOORLEYS
Print, Design & Publishing
info@moorleys.co.uk · www.moorleys.co.uk

Introduction

'Memory is the treasure house of the mind wherein the monuments thereof are kept and preserved'. Thomas Fuller

Welcome to this, my third collection of reminiscences from local folk.

I am extremely grateful to those former and present residents who have shared their memories with me. Without them this publication would not have been possible.

Herein are many wonderful stories, including coping with WWII, the floods of 1946-47, carnival days, schooling in the 40s to 60s, local farms and family businesses long gone. Much has changed in town and village life.

Despite much needed advances in many fields life seemed so much simpler before High Tech, Political Correctness and Health and Safety.

Hoping this will evoke memories for those of you of a certain age and for younger readers a peep into lives lived hereabouts in times gone by.

Happy reading!

Julia Powell
Editor
2019

CONTENTS

Page number

Breaston

01	The Youmans of Breaston	Karen Price
02	Breaston 1937 – 2018	Thelma Mortimer
05	Around the village with Cynthia Kent	Cynthia Kent
07	Breaston memories	Margaret McCaig and John Parker
10	Memories of Breaston	George Mounsey
13	Shirley Syson's Breaston	Shirley Syson
15	My memories of Breaston	Pam Smith
17	My Breaston memories	Pat Adcock (nee Philburn)
21	Margaret Whieldon's dog	Josephine Eaton

Draycott

22	Julia Hill's Draycott	Julia Hill
27	Our life in Draycott	Brian Reed
30	Footsteps of Neddytown	Janet Galer
32	Val Clare's Draycott	Val Clare

Long Eaton

34	My grandfather, Herbert Selwood	Keith Reedman
36	Long Eaton Weight Lifting Club	Lyndsey Fairbrother
38	Long Eaton Memories 1963 – 1972	Susan Halesworth

Sawley

40	My grandfather, James Frayne	Margaret Jennings
42	Mills Dockyard, Trent Lock, Sawley	Steve Mills
45	Memories of Sawley	Joan Rippengal (née Reedman)
56	The Tysoe's Sawley	Margaret and Frank Tysoe
60	John Hay-Heddle's Sawley	John Hay-Heddle
64	Memories of the floods in Sawley in 1947	Shirley Syson
65	Sawley and Long Eaton remembered	Jean Frearson
68	Memories of Carnival Day 1983	Jacqui Marshall

The Youmans of Breaston
By Karen Price

My great grandparent's surname was Youmans. Reuben was born on 22nd November 1886 and he moved to Long Eaton in 1910.

The following are some details regarding my great grandparents and their shop: -

Reuben Youmans was a stonemason by trade at Burton on Trent. At the age of 24 he moved to Long Eaton as a dairyman with his own milk round and developed his business, later moving to a farm on Blind Lane, Breaston. He and his wife Jessica had two daughters Winnie and Margaret. With the business expanding the family moved to 59 Risley Lane where, with his wife, he continued with the milk round and opened a general grocer's shop. They always called each other Reub and Jessie

The painting shown here is signed A. Plackett. It shows my great granny and grandad's shop on Risley Lane (view is looking down the lane in the direction of the Bulls Head).

BREASTON 1937 – 2018
By Thelma Mortimer

I grew up in Maylands Avenue, the only child of Syd and Elsie Hunt and first attended the Methodist Sunday School at the age of three. I was taken there by a girl called Hazel Daykin who also lived in the Avenue. In those days, there were houses to the east side of the Avenue only – the west side was gradually built on over the years. At this time, Maylands Avenue was an unmade road and all the girls regularly 'borrowed' one of their mother's clothes lines and played at skipping or ball, whips and tops, or hopscotch. There used to be a weekly visit by Mr Cartwright of Draycott with his horse and cart stocked with fruit and vegetables and non-perishable groceries – no plastic in those days. All the produce was loose, and a set of old-fashioned scales hung at the back of the cart. He announced his arrival by ringing a bell.

To the west side of the Avenue, there was a field with a short cut through the hedge to Breaston Park and a tennis court which belonged to the Harrisons who lived on the corner of the main road and the Avenue. This land is now Rectory Road and Cherry Close.

I started school at the age of five when the two infant classes were in St Michael's schoolroom. Miss Prince was the teacher of the reception class and Miss Lorimer taught the second class of the infants. There was an air raid shelter in the yard and I remember going into it in coat, scarf and gloves, carrying my gas mask, on two occasions. Also vividly remembered is one morning when, as usual, my mother took me to school, a very serious accident had just occurred where Risley Lane joins the main road. Three little boys who lived on Longmoor Lane had crossed Main Street behind a Barton's bus travelling towards Long Eaton. They had walked into the path of another bus travelling towards Derby. Two were badly injured and one of them was killed. Needless to say, it was a bad day in school. Following this incident, the bus stop to Derby was moved from outside St Michael's Church to its current position opposite The Bull's Head. A Zebra crossing was installed at the site of the accident and is now outside St Michael's Church.

Behind the bus stop was a farm and running parallel with the main road were brick-built pigsties. Along from them was a row of old cottages – long gone. The shop on the corner of Risley Lane was owned by Mrs Fearn, followed by Mrs French. It is now Bryn Farr's Hairdressers. Further along Main Street was the Post Office and a chip shop, the latter having moved from The Green. Bob Statham owned it and later it became a betting shop. It is now the Corner Deli.

After leaving Miss Lorimer's class, children moved to the Junior School in Sawley Lane, now Firfield School. Unfortunately, at this time, I caught Scarlet Fever which necessitated a six week stay in the isolation hospital in Hopwell Lane at Draycott. By the time I returned to school, I was in Miss Statham's class at the Junior School. Mr Percy Orrell was the headmaster, a very good teacher and a strict disciplinarian.

An old ad for Mrs Fearn's drapery

> Modern Underwear
> Smart Frocks
> Wools
>
> **Mrs. C. FEARN**
> General & Fancy Draper
> Main Street, Breaston
>
> New and
> Attractive Goods
> at Popular Prices.

I left Breaston School to attend Long Eaton Grammar School, where I stayed until the age of sixteen and then began my first job at British Celanese in the Acetone Recovery office. This position was obtained for me by my father who worked at Celanese just before he died in August 1953. In those days, the acetone was circulated in the air in the spinning department where my father worked. Later the company was bought by Courtaulds and great improvements were made to the conditions in the department, the liquid 'dope' being poured through pipes emerging as artificial silk. After a short time I moved to a position working in a bigger office, the Comptometer Bureau, for British Rail at Derby. I travelled by train from Breaston & Draycott Railway Station which sadly, was axed by Mr Beeching.

Breaston and Draycott Railway Station in its heyday

By this time, I had become a member of the Methodist Youth Club which initially met in the old chapel schoolroom, which is no longer there. It was in between Hogg's Bistro and Chapel Yard which was a collection of cottages. This site is now occupied by the Co-op. Prior to this, there were two Co-ops in Breaston – one in Blind Lane (now Anderson's) and one at the top of Woodland Avenue, now a bike shop. Land had been acquired for a new Methodist Hall in Risley Lane which was much later demolished, and the land became Manor Leigh and part of the Bull's Head car park. The Methodist Hall was incorporated into the Methodist Church building. It was at the Youth Club that I met my husband who, along with others, helped back stage at the many pantomimes which were staged annually. The pantos had an extremely good reputation and busloads of people travelled quite some distances to see them. They were written by Jack Astill, Harry Gray and Dennis Dodson, all three now deceased. These were happy days and lots of fun was had by all associated with the pantos.

From the age of twelve, I was trained as a singer by Mrs Doreen Gray and regularly sang the alto solos in Handel's Messiah which was performed annually by an augmented choir. There was an Eisteddfod held for the Long Eaton Free Churches in which I, along with others, competed. The Breaston Methodist Church choir, under the baton of Ruth Lawley, was outstanding in the area. Much later, I auditioned with Long Eaton Operatic Society and was accepted. My most outstanding memories are playing the role of Golde in 'Fiddler on the Roof' and exchange visits with Long Eaton's twin town of Langen in Germany. There our Society performed excerpts from shows to great acclaim by the locals. Many years ago, a Well Dressing was created outside the front of the Methodist Church and over the years the church has staged Flower Festivals with a Bible story theme. A very lively Christmas Market has also been held – both these events drawing many visitors from around and about the area.

Tony and I married in 1956 at the Methodist Church and our sons were born in 1962 and 1965 respectively. They also started their education at the Infants and Junior schools in Sawley Lane, moving to Western Mere School at eleven years of age. It was situated at the rear of the Hills Road Estate. It didn't have a sixth form so it was decided by Derbyshire County Council to close it and it was pulled down. Pupils had to relocate to Wilsthorpe School or Sandiacre Friesland. By that time my sons had left and taken up employment.

Breaston has increased in size over the years with the building of houses in Holmes Road, the joining of Belmont Avenue with Maylands, Willoughby Close, Belvoir Close and Meadow Close where we now live. The latter was built on land which was owned by Miss Cowing who had a smallholding surrounding a large house, which was pulled down to make room for our Close. Miss Cowing was involved with the Cubs and Scouts. She was also active in the Red Cross in the time of Dr Christie and the group met in a brick built converted barn which had stairs on the outside. This building was situated opposite Stevens Lane and was pulled down to make way for the bungalow which now occupies the site. During this time, the Post Office was situated in Main Street in the shop which is now 'Pretty Grey'. It eventually moved to its present position on The Green. It was housed in a new building which had its own sorting office at the rear. This building and the hairdressers next door replaced a row of old cottages which were demolished.

The inhabitants of Breaston are very fortunate to live in such a lovely village which, in the past two years, has been enhanced by 'Breaston in Bloom'. Flowers everywhere have been planted and nurtured by members of the W.I. and other volunteers. The result is a credit to all those involved in the project.

Around the village with Cynthia Kent
As told to Julia Powell

Cynthia was born in 1942 in a cottage in Chapel Yard. The cottages have long since gone and nowadays the Co-op supermarket stands in their place. The village was quite different in Cynthia's younger days from how it is today. Let her take us on a walk around.

Along Draycott Road the Breaston and Draycott Railway Station, which closed in 1966, was still open and there was a path to The Elms over the lines. There were one or two houses along the track to Sanderson's which was something to do with building aggregates. Then several more houses until the brook, a couple more houses then The Crescent on the council estate. I think there were eight houses on the front which were built after WWI. One of the houses along the front was a police house. There was another house and a shop, Wombwell's grocery and off sales was opposite The Golden Brook and then there were four more houses.

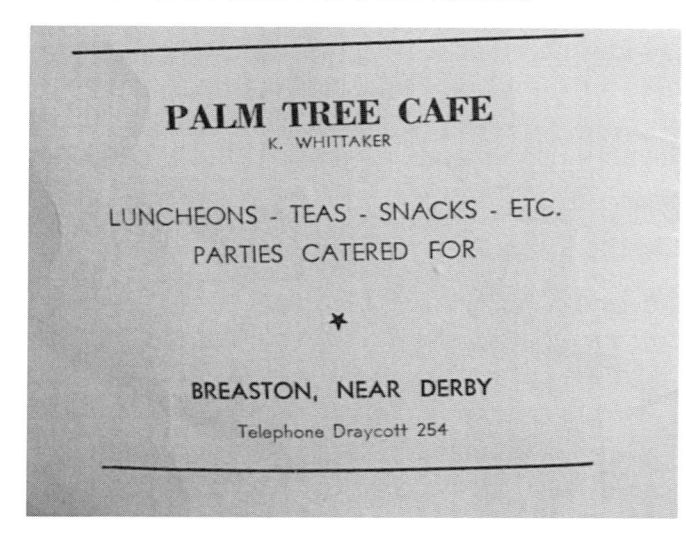

An early ad for the Palm Tree Cafe

There was a small café on Draycott Road run by Oswalds which was mainly used by commercial travellers. Later, around 1950 a larger room at the rear was built. The Palm Tree Café was mainly used for functions. It is now Finton's.

Hills Road Council Estate was built in the late 1940s and Festival Avenue was named after the Festival of Britain 1951. Western Mere School was there on Hind Avenue from around 1957 to 1990. It was demolished in 1992. There was a council building on Draycott Road, something to do with school dinners I believe. Middlestead House, 96 Draycott Road, is now a residential home. There were fields and a gate before the 'nasty bend' and four more houses before the brook. After that was Dr Christie's house, opposite Marlborough Road, and next-door Mrs Perk's house, then two more houses and two cottages.

After the café there was a path to fields then two houses and a small garage, which I think mainly did repairs. Behind that was The Cedars, home to Mrs Astle-Fletcher. It went down to fields at the back of Church House. There were two cottages, one owned by Jim Farrell and the other by Wilf Hales. The latter became Nurse Mitchell, the midwife's house.

When I was young Mr Cartwright used to come around with a horse and cart selling greengrocery. He kept his stock in a building on Draycott Road. Later he had a shop on Risley Lane. Miss Plackett, the village dressmaker lived in a cottage nearby.

On Main Street there was a farmyard, Warwick's Manor House and Ward's dairy, then Taylor's house where Dr Heddle had a surgery some days. Greenwoods, greengrocery, which was owned by Margaret Orchard's parents, Plackett's sweetshop and tobacconists and Arnold Smith's butcher's shop, later Cotton's now Dundas.

I remember Miss Harper's house on the corner of Steven's Lane, I think she was an artist. Moving along Main Street there was Oswalds grocers at number 48, then McGuires, then Reids. I remember folk who lived on The Terrace including Lucy Kent, the Godbers, Butlers and Haywoods. Roses had a greengrocery then it became Warringtons, then Kitchings. There was Bradley's house then another house and then Hogg's shoes and repairs. After that the Chapel Sunday School and Chapel Yard, Cobbler Gill's, whose shop front was on The Green, and Mrs Smith's on the corner. Statham's fish and chip shop was on The Green.

On The Green after the cobblers there were two houses, one became a hairdressers, then there was a house with a garden standing back where Fowkes lived. Where the Post Office now stands were two cottages, then a house and some small cottages around where Breaston Dental Care is now.

Beyond The Chequers one could find, amongst other premises, The Methodist Chapel, Clarke's barbers, the Post Office, Marsdens, Woodward's bakery and Mrs Fearn's haberdashery, now Bryn Farr the hairdresser. After The Bull's Head was Buxton's newsagents, Kind and Chambers the greengrocers, some houses, then wasteland with a path going through to the park. The parish church was and still is on the opposite side of the road together with the former St Michael's Schoolroom.

The Co-op grocery and butchers was on Blind Lane. This is now Anderson's. Along there is also Rose Cottage, formerly owned by The Plackett family, now a listed building.

The Firs on Steven's Lane was at one time a farmhouse, then a hotel and is now a residential home. Beyond that was, amongst other buildings, Jasmine Cottage and Stud Farm.

On Risley Lane there was the New Methodist School Room. I remember when it opened in 1953. There were huge celebrations for the Coronation. Kind and Chambers market gardeners were on Risley Lane and The Hawthorns, where Gaffer Wholey, a former headmaster at Breaston School, lived. There was a house and dairy on the lane owned by Ike Clay, the milkman and there was the Church Sunday School, which later became the library, also The Rectory which is now a care home.

An early photo of Mr Kind's delivery lorry

Apart from houses and cottages on Longmoor Lane I remember Paul's factory and a coal yard. Gambles farm and blacksmiths were on Ward's Lane.

Breaston memories
By Margaret McCaig and John Parker
As told to Julia Powell

Margaret started at Breaston School next to St Michael's Church in 1940 and remembers Miss Prince and Miss Lorimer. The toilets were across the yard, boys segregated from the girls. Not pleasant in freezing cold weather. There were tall trees around the playground and the kids used to make slides coming down from them. She recalls a child being killed on the crossing outside the school.

There were air raid shelters in the playing fields at the Firfield Avenue end and the children had to take gas masks for trial runs. When you were 7 you went to the big school on Sawley Lane. Mr Orrell and his wife were there. Then there was the scholarship and what was wrong in those days was they had the 'Honours Board' and it must have been so awful for the kids whose names weren't on it. Margaret passed the scholarship and went on to Nottingham Girls High School, some went to Long Eaton Grammar School and some went to Western Mere.

Margaret loved the wonderful aromas from Woodward's bakery. The shop was on Main Street but the ovens were at the rear on Blind Lane, approached by a jitty at the side of what is now Darling's opticians.

Memorial to Dr Christie

Beginning from around the 1940s the doctors in Breaston were Dr Donald, then Dr Christie followed by Dr Crompton. The surgery was in his house on Draycott Road, opposite the end of Marlborough Road. A flagpole in Breaston churchyard is dedicated to Dr Christie's memory. During the late 1970s the surgery moved to new premises on the Bridge Field Industrial Estate. In the 1940s and 50s before any of that was built a firm called Sanderson were on site making concrete products.

John was a butcher at Cotton's, now Dundas, on Main Street for around 20 years. One can still see the name of Joseph Plackett, who had it built, in the brickwork on one side of the shop. Down one side there were pig sties and the slaughterhouse for the butcher's shop.

43 Main Street was Warwick's farm house. They had a few cows and they grew potatoes up near the cemetery on Longmoor Lane. John used to go potato picking there. They had a huge carthorse called Charlie which often went wild. The farmer would come up Longmoor Lane with the horse and cart but if Charlie took the hump he would charge and you would see Warwick running after it trying to catch it.

Mrs Ward lived at The Manor House on Main Street and in that yard was a dairy from where they operated a milk round. All the outbuildings are housing now. The same family had a chip shop up the road.

Where the parish council rooms on Blind Lane are situated there used to be a horticultural society which sold seed potatoes and other garden supplies. A R Smith, aka Brickie Smith, had his office on Wards Lane and his builder's yard was around where Cresswell's was of late.

Where the Holmes Road estate is now was Clowes Farm, off Stevens Lane. Opposite the end of Stevens Lane was a converted barn once used by the Red Cross and St John's Ambulance Brigade. Margaret's father used to attend the St John's classes there with Tommy Beadling

The church ran a youth club and there were cubs and scouts groups in a wooden hut on Dale Close, now they have a brick building behind Anderson's. The chapel used to put on a pantomime every year which was very popular. Stan Ruff often had a leading part.

Miss Watson lived at The Hollies and was very well known along with her geese, which used to make a mess everywhere and could be dangerous. When she went to church they would wait outside for her. She donated Duffield Close, the field which is now the village green, to the village in perpetuity. That is where the annual May Day Fete is held.

John recalls that originally there was a wall around The Chequers pub and it used to stick out halfway into the middle of the road. It was very narrow between it and the church lych gate and there were cobblestones all around.

The Bull's Head goes back a long way. It used to be all little tiny rooms and there are beams in there from old sailing ships. On Risley Lane there is a hatch which is where the draymen used to offload beer barrels. John used to play with the landlord's lad when he was at primary school around the 1950s. Margaret remembers the dalmatian belonging to Mary Chambers stealing the landlord's Sunday joint and running around the village with the leg of lamb.

Margaret and John remember kids swimming in the canal and jumping off the bridge near the Navigation Inn. When John was at secondary school a section of the canal was cleaned out and re-established as a swimming pool. There weren't any boats on it by then.

John remembers when the Co-op used to deliver bread on Tuesdays and Thursdays and milk every day. The bread came from their Fletcher Street bakery. They also brought trays of cakes and you could order your Christmas pork pies etc. There was also a coal round, the order having been placed at the Co-op in Blind Lane. Another Co-op shop was on the corner of Woodland Avenue where the bike shop is now. Margaret recalls Mr Youmans who used to come around with the milk in a churn. A rag and bone man with a horse and cart also used to call.

A fair used to come to The Green twice a year but that was when The Green was where the car park is now. Sometimes a circus would also come.

Billy Paul had a factory on Longmoor Lane manufacturing kitchen sink and cabinet units, washing machines, paraffin heaters, canteen equipment, parts for Rolls-Royce jet engines and all types of stainless-steel fabrications. The business was acquired by Glynwed in 1972. Billy kept racing cars at what is now The Farm Shop.

In 1957 Harrimans Drive was still a field with a farm track down it and the village used to have football and cricket matches in the field. John used to play with the lads from The Bull's Head and the landlady used to make an enamel bucket full of coffee with a bottle of rum in it for the footballers to drink at half time and the lads would have to carry it down to the field. There would be Boxing Day matches against local teams and many were formed in the local pubs. Breaston Tigers would play versus Draycott Donkeys.

Margaret used to go potato picking at Ilsley's farm which was at Wilsthorpe Island. There used to be a herd of pigs on one corner of the island. On the other side was Baron's nursery where Eaton Farm is now. The building stood back with a long track from the road and they used to sell roses. John recalls there were 3 prefabs around there and one of his relations used to live in one.

When you walked from Long Eaton to Breaston in those days it was all fields and before the motorway there was a row of trees.

Memories of Breaston
By George Mounsey

Breaston County School in the late 40s to mid 50s

Miss Prince was your first teacher. My only memory was playing with sand and shells. Miss Lorimer would draw a star in your book if your writing was good. Miss Mellors was quite strict. There were musical instruments and I played a triangle. I don't think I was her favourite. Of Miss Gould I have no memory.

The former Breaston County Primary School

I remember Mr Byrne, an Irishman, who was very strict. I believe he married the cookery teacher. Mr Heeks ran the football team. We played on Breaston Park and he would take us swimming in Derby. Mrs Orrell tried to show you how to write correctly and she taught the children about to take the 11 plus exam. On Monday morning you paid 5 shillings (25p) for your week's school meal. Mr Whitehouse would read wonderful stories, but he used to give us the cane. Mrs Quinn looked after the girls netball team. If you behaved in class, she would reward you with an éclair.

The class rooms were heated by a coke fired boiler. I think the guy who shovelled the coke was Mr Percy Rose. We used to lock him in the boiler house.

Mr Strong was the last teacher before you left school. His classroom was also used as the room to provide the children with hot dinners. The smell of cabbage would prevail for the rest of the day.

To give children an idea of working we visited local businesses including Boots and Stanton Iron Works, where we watched molten iron being poured. Also, we went to the railway workshops at Derby, Long Eaton Advertiser, and Shipley colliery. Health and Safety was unheard of then. We descended into the pit in a cage, still wearing our school clothes. The colliers were unhappy as they had to wait to ascend the pit after a hard shift. Some choice swear words!

The cookery classroom and the woodwork room were used by both Breaston and Draycott pupils. Miss Curry and Mr Slack were the teachers. I don't think anyone had heard of curry in those days otherwise the teacher Miss Curry would have had to put up with some ribbing.

We were given a small, third of a pint, bottle of milk free each day. Older children would carry the crates of milk to each classroom. We had regular visits by the nit nurse and if you had lice you were given a brown envelope to pass to your parents. Teeth were inspected and you were sent to the clinic in Long Eaton, which was a frightening experience.

There were seasonal games played at school, Whip and Top, Conkers, making slides on the ice etc. On the school field there were air raid shelters, but I don't know if they were ever used.

All children walked to school. No parking problems in those days! The teachers did not own cars either. Halloween was unheard of. To celebrate Christmas children would bring sandwiches and cake to eat in the classroom. In 1953, when it was the Queen's Coronation, we were all given a mug!

Shops, pubs and the GP.

In the early fifties the publicans at the Navigation Inn were Ben and Ruby. They kept St Bernard dogs. If you were small enough Ruby would let you have a ride on the dogs' backs. They also had a parrot; its cage was situated in what was nicknamed Polly's room. In another room there was a crib table. When the men were playing a game, they would tap on the table for Ruby to take their order for beer. There used to be a small serving hatch. If you ordered a pint Ben would pass it out and in a very deep voice, he would say loudly "One and nine" (about 8pence in new money). The prices stayed the same for years. The gentlemen's conveniences were situated outside, adjacent to the canal and were difficult to negotiate in the dark. I can't recall what the ladies used.

The doctor's surgery was on Draycott Road, opposite Marlborough Road. The GP was Dr Christie a Scotsman. Access to the waiting room was at the side of the house, it was not a big room and I recall Mrs Marks was the receptionist. There were upright chairs placed around the walls and there was a big clock which had a loud tick. The doctor would sew a wound up and if needed apply a sling. No appointments were necessary.

Mrs Wombwell kept an off licence on Draycott Road just past Marlborough Road. I think it was the only shop open in the evenings.

The cobbler's shop, now Hoggs Bistro belonged to Mr Norman Hogg who repaired shoes. I used to take my football boots to have new segs fitted for sixpence (two and a half pence). Mr and Mrs Kitching kept a greengrocery shop on Main Street. It's a hairdresser now. Mr Kitching had a large allotment off Harrimans Drive and grew most of the produce.

There was a tiny sweet shop next door to Dundas the butchers. I can't recall the name of the gentleman who owned it. He used scales and would weigh out the quantities one requested. I remember he had a disability and wore an enormous boot due to one of his legs being shorter than the other.

Ken Clarke kept a men's hairdressing shop. This was where the fish and chip shop is now located on Main street. Mr Statham kept the chip shop on the Green. Mr Woodward ran a bakery on Main Street. You could buy a cob for a penny.

What is now the chemist's shop on Wilsthorpe Road used to be Buxton's the newsagent. The Long Eaton Advertiser was delivered on Friday afternoons by the paper boys. Payment was an old shilling (5pence) and a packet of crisps. If your parents had a regular paper delivered, you could buy a quarter of mint imperials and ask Mr Buxton to put the cost on the weekly paper bill if you were brave enough.

There were two spinsters, the Flowers, who kept a small grocery shop on Longmoor Lane, adjacent to the jitty leading to Belmont Avenue. I recall they owned a small car which was not common in those days. Another grocery shop on the corner of Maxwell Street was owned by a Mr Ridgeway.

For many years the landlord of the Chequers was Jabez Wright. I sat next to their son George at school. The pub was very popular and had a pianist on a Sunday night. Where Andersons cafe is now used to be the Co-op. One of the assistants was a girl called Marilyn and she used to smother me in kisses when I was a child. I remember using a ration book to purchase food. You bought the milk and bread tokens at this shop. The products were delivered by horse and cart. If the horse decided to use the toilet while at your property you were sent out with a bucket and shovel and then threw the manure on the garden.

Shirley Syson's Breaston
As told to Julia Powell

I was born in Mablethorpe but when the war broke out mum brought us to Sawley as there was bombing expected along the coast. I have been in this house in Breaston for 40 years since it was built. Before that I lived at Hays Avenue until my mum got married again. I was married in Breaston Church in 1958 by Canon Pemberton. My husband Gordon died in 2016.

There used to be two privately owned little buses running around Long Eaton, Sawley and up to Breaston. When I was about 7 my mum used to take us to the Navigation Inn on Risley Lane to meet a friend from Long Eaton and we would sit outside, me with a lemonade. Ruby, who was at the pub then, used to get St Bernard dogs from the monastery at Staunton Harold and there are actually two buried under the lawns at the Navi. She had three all together over the years and used to give them Yorkshire puddings. Eventually Ruby ended up with a Pekinese, which she had lying in state on a cushion when he died.

I spent a lot of time when I started riding around age 15 with my friends who lived on Beech Avenue off Poplar Road. Brenda and Pat had a riding school at the top of Wilsthorpe Road. We used to go to horse shows together. There used to be three farms up there before the motorway came. Around the mid-1950s a butcher from Sawley called Ken used to breed pigs in one of the stables and once he asked me if I could help him take them down to the field on Petersham Road. Of course, it wasn't built on then. There must have been about a hundred including the piglets and three or four of us herded them all the way down there. It took ages. After about two hours I suddenly said to Ken 'Look what's coming back down the road!' The pigs were all going back on their own.

Old ad for W. H. Paul Limited

My husband Gordon was brought to live in Breaston in 1940 and he used to tell me lots of tales. He worked at Billy Paul's factory on Longmoor Lane. They used to make sheet metal, sinks and cookers etc.

There used to be a cobbler on the main road called Cobby Gill. When Gordon was in one day collecting his shoes, a fellow came in and asked if his shoes were ready to collect. Cobby replied that they weren't quite ready but would be in a couple of hours. When the man had gone Cobby told Gordon it was a good job he hadn't looked down because Cobby was wearing his shoes.

On the other side of the road where Pidcock's motorcycles is now there was a garage owned by Billy Murden. He drove his Rolls Royce just a few yards up the road to The Chequers for a drink. There used to be a saddlery where Breaston Dental Care is now. The Co-op was on Blind Lane and then a bookie where Anderson's is now. There was a good quality second hand clothing shop at 48 Main Street where Margaret Fearn also did alterations and soft furnishings.

The Farm shop used to be a smallholding. Bill Cotton lived next door to the farm shop and he was the butcher before Dundas. He owned fields at the back of the farm shop, and he said people didn't know it but there was a footpath through his land He didn't advertise that.

In the 1950s one of the locals decided to hold a goose raffle. He touted the dead bird around the pubs whilst having a few pints along the way. However, by the time he'd finished dragging it through the streets by the neck the goose wasn't in a fit state to be given as a prize. Who knows what happened to the ticket money!

Around the same period there was an amusing incident regarding a Barton's Double Decker. The last bus of the day from Derby arrived in Breaston one evening, but when the conductor counted the passengers, he decreed that five would have to get off, as there were too many aboard. Nobody was willing to leave so apparently the conductor said he was going for a cuppa but when he got back, he expected there would be five less passengers. As soon as he had gone someone rang the bell and the driver set off. In those days he would be in a separate cab and would not have known that the conductor was no longer aboard. Presumably the bus travelled all the way to Nottingham until the driver realised he had lost his conductor.

Up until about twenty-five years ago it was a haven of wildlife around here. There were hares, hedgehogs, shrews, crickets etc. The brook was full of fish and newts, but modern farming methods have sadly put an end to that.

There was a canal basin behind The Navigation and a hump backed bridge went over the road, but the canal was filled in during the 1960s because it was going to cost as much to clean it out as to fill it in. Since 1994, there has been a restoration project spearheaded by the Derby and Sandiacre Canal Trust.

My late husband Gordon used to live in Mount Street and there was a footpath from Belmont Avenue through to Longmoor Lane. There were allotments all the way along before it was built on. Once when Gordon was going along there with three pals the first chap said he was going to nab one of the cabbages for his missus. It would be dark when they came back so he put a white paper bag over a really nice cabbage. However, the chap at the back took it off and put it on a grotty one. The wife wasn't impressed when she received it.

A gang of us would meet up with our dogs and one of the gang was Arthur Nicholls. He used to keep retired greyhounds or whippets. Sadly, his wife got killed on the crossing on Main Street.

On the triangle as you come into Holmes Road there used to be a blacksmith. The building is no longer there. Where the petrol station is now was a garden nursery. They had a magpie on the counter who would talk to you.

I used to keep two horses down on the farm on Sawley Lane when it was Mr Powdrill's. When the Motorway planners came to his farm he sent them off with a rifle in his hand.

One of the dairy farms round here used to sell milk to the Co-op. There were stiles across the fields and the cows would come and greet you, even the bull. When the farmer got a new bull he said it wasn't to be trusted.

My memories of Breaston
By Pam Smith

My memories of Breaston begin from December 1955 when, together with my parents, I moved into a house on Wilsthorpe Road, just along from The Bull's Head. At that time, it was almost possible to be completely self-sufficient in the village as the many shops covered everything needed to feed and keep a family.

Along from us was Chambers fruit and vegetable shop, now C2 Hairdesign. Chambers also sold garden implements and were helped in the shop by their daughter Mary, who married Derek Clowes. She also ran the garden nursery on Risley Lane, now Manor Leigh, and had a chicken farm and several goats. I remember her being angry that she wasn't allowed to sell the goat's milk. However, she could give it away.

Next to Chambers was a general grocery store owned by Tommy Buxton, a most amiable man. He also sold newspapers and you could buy anything from him from a sweeping brush to a bobbin of cotton. The shop is now Evans Pharmacy.

On the corner, opposite The Bull's Head, was a small haberdashery shop run by Mrs Elm, later taken over by Mrs French, now Bryn Farr's hairdressers. Further up Risley Lane was a general grocer's shop owned and run by Jack Elm. My mother ordered her weekly groceries from him and a delivery boy on a bicycle brought them to the door. That shop is now Nail Perfection by Natalie.

The double fronted shop formerly Cache Pot, now Pretty Grey, used to be the post office in one half and a hardware store in the remainder. This was run by the Woolley family. My father bought the oil for the Paul Warmer from there. The heater was made in W. H. Paul's factory on Longmoor Lane. Later the Woolleys moved to The Square when the new post office and store was built.

The Paul Warmer

Another important man in the village was Ken Clarke, the local barber. He had several different premises, one being the take away near the chapel. On retirement he moved to a house on Ward's Lane and converted the bottom end of the garage to a salon with huge mirrors on the walls. I know this because my husband and I bought the house from him in 1969.

Statham's chip shop was in The Square. I think they only opened at night. Years later it moved to the main road.

Where JKL Hairdressers is now has, in the past, been a cycle shop and small garage, Samuel Hogg boot maker and boot and shoe repairer, then a greengrocer run by the Kitching family. Hogg's son Richard moved the shoe shop and repairs to the shop that is now Hogg's Bistro.

A further shop on the corner of Stevens Lane was a small grocer. They also ran a taxi business but sadly the owner had a fatal accident one day whilst repairing his car. The business then became No 48, where Margaret Fearn sold best quality nearly new clothes

and made to measure curtains. There was also a small café at the back run by her daughter Sally.
On the opposite side of the road was Cotton's butcher's shop, now Dundas, and a small hairdresser. A second butcher's shop was in the Co-operative Store, now Andersons.

We also had a library on Risley Lane, which had limited opening times and in my memory the librarian was Jean Crisp. Across the lane from the library was another grocery shop owned by Bob Cartwright and his family.

The village shops closed daily for a lunch hour and on Wednesday afternoons. A far cry from today's open all hours supermarkets.

At the end of Blind Lane was The Hollies where Polly Watson, of a well-known Breaston family, lived. She kept geese which were always escaping and wandering around The Square and close to the bus stop, near the main road.

My Breaston memories
By Pat Adcock (nee Philburn)

1960 Marriage and Wilsthorpe School Journeys

In 1960 Maurice and I had just married and were living in a flat at the Old Vicarage in Breedon Street, Long Eaton. Most people started off in a small house, but we were trying to save money in order to buy one to begin with. Our rent was £4 a week. The cost of houses was going up as fast as our savings, but we had begun to look around. We found a house on the main road in Breaston which intrigued us because it was Art Deco and built in 1935. It was called The Spinney, because it was surrounded by poplar trees and had been the last one in the road before the more modern houses next door had been built. In April Maurice and I took a party of girls from Wilsthorpe School on holiday to Heidelberg. With Nancy Myatt, Jean Cowell and Glenis Barlow I had organised the first trip abroad in 1959 when we went to Bacharach on the Rhine. The cost was £25 per head and parents made sacrifices to give their children an opportunity to go abroad, something that they could not have afforded themselves. On our return in 1962, we decided to look seriously at the house and made an offer. It was for sale at £3500 but there was no way we could afford that. In those days my salary as a teacher was not counted against a mortgage. Nor did I receive equal pay with men teachers.

Moving to Breaston

There was a pay telephone in the flats, but this was only for outgoing calls. A note was put through the letterbox from the estate agents saying that if we could pay another £50 more than our offer then the house would be ours. I can't remember where we found the £50 from, certainly not from our parents, but eventually we moved into 29 Wilsthorpe Road on the 13th of July 1962. There was much to do as an old widower, Mr Manning, had been living here on his own and neglected the garden. As the property was owned by Perks, they had decorated it throughout and I remember blue cabbage roses in the lounge. A cine camera was a luxury in those days, but we had one because Maurice decided to stop smoking in order to buy one. Thus, we have film of all our lives from this date and the start of a lifelong hobby. We had very little furniture to move into the house, a bed, one carpet, a table, four chairs and two armchairs. My bicycle was leaning against the lounge wall. Very close to the house was an extremely large magnolia tree, which attracted a great deal of attention when it started to blossom. Since then they have become very popular and are no longer rare. We changed the name to Magnolia House.

The Magnolia Tree

I met Mr Siddalls, who had one of the first garden centres, where the petrol station now is. He told me that he planted the Magnolia Soulangeana, advising Mrs Manning that the place where she wanted it was far too close to the house. That was only about a yard away and facing south. She insisted that was where it had to go. Many years later, as the tree grew higher than the house, we reluctantly decided to cut it down. The temperature in the lounge increased by 2°. However, we did replace it by a much smaller Magnolia Stellata, so the name plaque we had bought could still stay the same.

Car ownership.

We had been moving smaller items in a brand-new Austin A40 deluxe saloon car in horizon blue, fitted with a heater and screen washer. It cost £678. The money from this came from Barclay's Bank. Maurice had been the proud owner of a drop head Sunbeam Talbot car, which looked beautiful but, because it was old was not reliable for his new job at the Electricity Board. He was required to provide his own vehicle. As my father Gilbert Philburn had been a car mechanic, I had been lucky to ride in his cars, such as the Austin 7. Before she died in 1976, my mother Lena used to say, "I can remember when there were only two cars parked in Curzon Street."

My driving test 1956

I learnt to drive while I was teaching at Longmoor Junior Boys' School where I had forty-four seven-year-olds in the first class that I taught. The driving test was scheduled for a Saturday morning but, two days before, I received a letter saying that all driving tests had been cancelled because of the Suez crisis. However, I was allowed to drive solo provided I kept my L plates on. When I eventually passed my test at Loughborough, it was an exciting day in my life. My father had taught me to handle the car and a friend taught me to pass the driving test. Petrol was scarce and expensive so most of us used bicycles as transport.

Shopping at the butcher's

I used to buy meat from Bill Cotton at the corner shop which now belongs to the Dundas family. I bought a tongue from him one Christmas which I boiled and pressed myself. I recall that he once told me that I was the first woman he had seen in a trouser suit. This was a time when women teachers were forbidden to wear trousers. I had bought the matching orange trousers, jacket and skirt from C and A at Nottingham.

> **Weights and Prices from the Past**
>
> When I gave up teaching at Wilsthorpe School to look after my daughter Jennifer, we had to rely on my husband's income alone, so I had to be careful how much money I spent on food. I recently found my accounts of what I spent at Bill Cotton's butcher's shop (now Dundas) on 10th April 1965 which made interesting reading as the total bill came to exactly one pound.
>
> | | | |
> |---|---|---|
> | ¾ lb best sausage | 2s 10d | (14p) |
> | ½ lb second steak & ¼ lb kidney | 3s 5d | (17p) |
> | ½ lb collar bacon | 1s 10d | (9p) |
> | 2 lamb chump ends | 2s | (10p) |
> | ¼ lb tongue | 2s 6d | (12½p) |
> | ½ lb pork sausage | 1s 8d | (8½p) |
> | 10 oz fillet steak | 5s 9d | (29p) |
>
> *[The modern currency equivalents are in brackets. Ed.]* In those days there were 12 pence ("d") in one shilling (=5p nowadays) and 20 shillings ("s") in a pound. Then as now, there were 16 ounces ("oz") in one pound weight ("lb"), which is a bit under half a kilogram.

Wilsthorpe Secondary Modern School

During my years when I was aged 22 to 28 at Wilsthorpe Secondary Modern School, the school population was decimated by the Asian flu epidemic. There were no free periods and if I were rescheduled to replace the full time P.E. teacher, then I would go into the changing room, tell the girls to get changed and then teach them; whether it was outdoor games or gym. So I was switched to full-time PE, because it was better to get the girls outside in the fresh air and other staff took my classroom lessons until normal lessons resumed. I was able to wear a track suit and my beloved Dunlop Green Flash plimsolls, but women were expected to wear skirts.

I played hockey for Long Eaton Nomads and enjoyed teaching tennis, staying after school to get longer use of the courts in the summer months. One year I organised a visit to Wimbledon tennis championships and took twenty girls. Because the M1 had not reached Long Eaton, it took a long time to make the journey by coach. Wilsthorpe Road, close to the island had to be re-configured in order for a bridge to be built where the M1 would pass below.

I retired from Wilsthorpe School in July 1964 when I was pregnant. For those of us who lived in this area a most interesting thing to do was to stand and stare at the vehicles required to move land to create space for the M1 motorway.

Teaching after pregnancy.

Jennifer was born in February 1965. Because I did not expect to be able to teach again, I concentrated on being a housewife and a gardener. Also I looked after my widowed mother living in Curzon Street. One day the headmistress of Wellington Street Infant School, Miss Cordingley, came to see me in desperation. She needed an extra member of staff for the summer term as the numbers always increased then. This was the school that I myself had attended as an infant. I pointed out to her that I had my own little girl to look after. She said "How old is she? " I replied, "Three years old." She said, "Bring her with you".

My classroom was the corridor, as this was the only space left. Thus, it was that in 1969 I was teaching the first child to whom I could say, "I taught your mother". One thing I remember teaching them was about the moon landing, which has always fascinated me. Jennifer sat behind me on my bicycle on a special seat bought for the purpose. At this time of course, there were not many cars on the roads.

Breaston on cine film

Maurice and I have made a record of Breaston since 1962 starting with 8 mm to which we had to add sound. The Parish Council has ensured that parishioners were consulted over several matters. They bought Duffield Close, which is now used for the Annual Gala. Later the paths were improved by Manpower Services and I remember making a special point that they should not be in straight lines.

Schools

When I first came to Breaston in 1962 there were two schools, Western Mere Secondary Modern school on the Hills Road Estate and Firfield Primary School (renamed in 1966) down Firfield Avenue. Eventually I taught at Firfield and tried in vain, as part of a team, to save Western Mere from being closed down. The old brick part of the former Breaston County School was built in 1913 and I was there in 1988 when we celebrated the schools 75th anniversary. I have a very interesting booklet which was created at the time when Lynne Crockett was chairman of the governors. This is a very detailed souvenir and I note from this that I had already been at the school for 15 years. In 1973 I was approached by the head John Rigby (1966 - 1983) with whom I had taught at Longmoor Junior Boys (1956-1958) because he needed a teacher to take a class in the dining room, which was near to Sawley Road. A kitchen and new hall to be used for assemblies and as a dining room/gymnasium were going to be constructed, but at the time there were more pupils than space.

Firfield Primary School. Part of the original building.

So, I moved in with twenty shoeboxes for the children to use for their pencils et cetera, because there were only tables and chairs in the room. Gradually we acquired more appropriate furniture. The problem was that at 11.30 the dinner ladies required the room so I had to move out. Because my first-year juniors, aged seven, were small, I was able to fit them into the staffroom or, if the weather was good, we would sit outside on the grass. On one memorable occasion I asked permission to take the children to my house, so that we could watch the last episode of a television programme in colour. The school television was also based in my classroom, but it was only black and white at this time. There was a suggestion that the school might have a maypole and as I was involved with girls sport, I had to take on the task. As it had sixteen ribbons, I invented a system using the points of the compass, so that the children knew precisely where they were in relation to each other. Much practising went into the final presentation at several summer fairs.

Gradually more alterations were made to the school buildings and in 2019 it is now completely different, but the old part still remains. Unfortunately, that is not the case with Western Mere Secondary School, which although more modern than Firfield had been bulldozed. When I was offered early retirement at the age of 58 I was loath to accept because I thoroughly enjoyed my teaching career at Firfield School. The advent of computers was embraced by me and I was absolutely fascinated by this. I also liked the Christmas period when it was possible to put on a nativity play with words written by the children. I have videos and photographs of a lot of my time there, including my last day at school when my class was responsible for Assembly. Later in the day the head teacher Mr Ellison called me to the phone, because the office wanted to speak to me. I might have presumed that they wanted to thank me for my contribution to education in the local area, but I would have been wrong. They were pointing out that I had been overpaid by a week and I should send them a cheque for this money.

Margaret Whieldon's dog
By Josephine Eaton

Margaret was the much-loved organist for many years at St Michael's, Breaston. This is the story of 'Bubbles' and how she acquired her.

Right from the start 'Bubbles' had a special place in Margaret's heart, the dog she adopted through a charity specialising in finding new homes for unwanted dachshunds.

The organisation of the handover sounds a little haphazard. Apparently, the dog was still with the original owner, who lived up north. It was decided that the easiest way would be for the owner and Margaret to meet at a motorway service station, halfway between the two addresses.

As Margaret eagerly approached the car, which contained 'Bubbles', the dour faced owner roughly scooped up the dog and handed it over, with just one comment. "Its name is Bubbles." Naturally Margaret was expecting to have a chat about the dog's feeding habits etc but there was no opportunity. The woman got back into her car and drove away. Margaret was flabbergasted. Then she felt her new charge trembling in her arms. As she tenderly stroked her, she discovered the unkempt fur and general air of neglect.

A friend drove them back to Long Eaton and Margaret spent the journey soothing and reassuring her new pet. When they arrived home one of Margaret's immediate tasks was to groom the tiny dog, measuring about 18 inches long, with a height of about 9 inches. She had a beautiful black silky coat, flecked with gold.

Over the following months Margaret gradually trained the pet and built up its confidence and Bubbles became a devoted companion, accompanying Margaret wherever possible. They usually travelled by car but sometimes on buses or trains when on holiday. As Bubbles grew older and was unable to walk far Margaret was undeterred and bought her a pushchair. The two companions became familiar figures at the local park, where the dog was able to take gentle exercise on the grass. During the summer they sometimes caught the train into the Peak District with Margaret's friends, who took turns with the pushchair.

Eventually Margaret took the heart-breaking decision to have the little dog put to sleep. She confided that sometimes she felt 'Bubbles' presence nearby, which enhanced her happy memories of the tiny dog.

Julia Hill's Draycott.
As told to Julia Powell.

Julia was born on the 11th of September 1939 just after WW2 broke out. This is her story.

My first memory of Draycott was hearing a siren and we all had to go in one room where a blast wall had been built in front of the window. Me and my parents and my granny used to go and sit in there while an air raid was on.

My dad was an Irishman and worked as a bricklayer. When I was a little girl, he used to take me on walks and taught me a lot about nature and wildlife. I think that is why I grew up to really enjoy that. I can remember going down to a brook at Wilne to get watercress. The water was very clean then.

Wilne now is not the old one I knew with the cowsheds, Mr Wood's farm and the cottages. You could go and sit in Mrs Smith's garden and drink her homemade lemonade. Mrs Broad was born at Wilne and lived to be 106. I made her 100th birthday cake.

Church Lane, Wilne in times gone by.

One of my earliest memories, I could only have been about 4 years of age, was of my mother working on the land for Mr Beswick. Of course, a lot of the men had gone to war. The farm had a big shire horse called Captain and a hay cart. Us children would often go up with our mothers and hang about in the fields while the work was being done. When it was time to bring the hay down the lane, to put it into the big barn, us kids used to scramble on to the cart and hang on the back. The gentleman who drove the horse was Mr Holt and he used to shout "Owdger, Owdger" which I think meant hold on.

When the war finished, we had a big bonfire on a field near us and I can remember somebody dragging a piano out to play into the middle of Walter Street. They brought tables out and for the first time I can remember sitting having chips. There were houses in three streets around where I lived, built on land that had belonged to Jack Skerritt. He had a lace factory in Walter Street. The factory has recently been pulled down for housing. We lived in Gertrude Road which was named after Miss Skerritt and then there was Walter Street and Arthur Street named after other family members.

I went to Sunday school from when I was 3 at St Mary's in Draycott, which belonged to St Chads. It's now in what was the Wesleyan Chapel. When I was little it was in Garfield Avenue. When I was old enough, I joined the choir and was still in it when I got married. I also belonged to the youth club and that's where Vicar Boden got us interested in history

I can remember as vivid as anything my mum taking me to my first day at school. At the end of Hopwell Lane there used to be a very big beech tree and I was always a bit afraid of big trees because of the leaves rustling. As we set off my granny gave me a penny, which would buy me a few sweets when I came home. She said she was giving me it because I was starting school and she wanted me to be a good girl. Unfortunately, when

I passed under the beech tree, which frightened me, I began to run and dropped my penny down a drain. Years after I was walking my cousin Peggy, who was in a wheelchair, along the lane and I remarked to her that every time I passed that drain it reminded me of my lost penny.

I remember Mrs Frith in my first class. She was a lovely lady. Then there was Miss Wilson and Miss Hill, three teachers in the juniors. Then we went up into what we called the Big School from around ages 10 to 15, with Mrs Wooliscroft. If you ever asked anyone who went to Draycott School if they could remember Mrs Wooliscroft then they would recall how we feared her. She was very strict. She had brown hair and her clothes always seemed to be brown too, jumper, skirt handbag etc. She would stand at the door telling us to "Come along, with no messing about."

There were no cookery facilities at Draycott School, so we used to have to go down to a big long prefab on Firfield Avenue, Breaston. The girls learned cookery and washing and ironing in one part and the boys had woodwork and metalwork in the other part. We came back on a bus and the lads would be eager to know what we had been making. Half the cakes and things we made never came home!

I used to play on the cricket field, and it was safe then. As I got older, we'd play at jumping the brook off Hopwell Lane. If you fell in all you did was tip the water out of your wellies and put them back on.

When the village school had been open 100 years they were asking people who had lived in Draycott for certain periods if they would like to go and talk to the children. I was there from 1945 to 1955 so I went and spoke to them. Afterwards they were invited to ask questions. A little boy's hand shot up and he asked, "Please Miss, were there buses when you were little?" I think he thought I was born in the era of stagecoaches! Several people went to talk to the children, and it was a really enjoyable afternoon.

I got scarlet fever in 1947 but I had to stay at home, and they had to keep spraying the room. I couldn't go to the hospital because there was that much snow that year you couldn't get up there. They say you could nearly walk on the edge tops. Afterwards the hospital became a place where patients recuperated after surgery. It's now part of a housing development.

The old canal cottages

Opposite Nooning Lane, opposite the old railway bridge there was a gap in the hedge where the donkeys used to go and offload their coal onto the barges. This was when the Derby Canal went from Sandiacre Locks into Derby. My cousin Brenda and two of her children were born in one of the now derelict cottages up there. Derby and Sandiacre Canal Trust have purchased the cottages and are restoring them. They used to call it the Golden Mile up there. You went up Hopwell Lane and there was a little bridge, one way went to Breaston the other to Derby.

When I became interested in history, I found out about the old cinder pad. It was called a pad because many years ago, it was the way the packhorses used to go over the ford at Wilne to go into South Derbyshire. There was a big old mill there used for cotton spinning. When I was a little girl you could go through the yard and pay a penny to Mr Wilmot, who lived in the toll house, to go over a bridge and then we used to paddle in the shallows there on the other side. We thought we'd been to Blackpool!

Old Mrs Astle used to live at Attewell House. The family were lace people. I helped at their garden parties and would always put on my best frock for the afternoon. The church always had their summer fair there and served teas and ice creams. Also hand knitted woollens and other items were on sale. I remember the gardens were absolutely beautiful. There was a big rose garden at the side going almost down to Sawley Road. The site of it is now Attewell Close.

Marcus Astle lived in Attewell House at one time. He was a manufacturer who owned the old Wilne Mill, where they did cotton spinning and doubling. Once when I was in the youth club the ghost of Marcus Astle was mentioned. He was supposed to walk in Wilne churchyard on a certain night of the year. I think it was sometime in March. Anyway, about eight of us, including Derek Orchard and Steve and Jean Godber, went down one night. There was a lot of giggling and fooling about amongst the gravestones. Then all at once there was ever such a funny noise and I've never seen anybody move as quickly as we did. We didn't see a ghost, but several locals had said they'd seen something strange down there.

From Wilne to Sawley used to be what they called the Roman Road. I went out with a local farmer, Peter Nash, at one time and his gran and grandad lived in the old farm halfway along the road. Whenever I used to go down to meet Peter, with my dog Timmy, as soon as we got to a certain stile the dog's ears and fur went up and it wouldn't go that way. Peter told me there had apparently been a murder along there and the dog sensed something.

If you come up Sawley Lane, there's a triangular bit where it meets the main road. Years ago, it was the village pound with a fence around it. If there were stray cattle they would be kept there, until the farmer came to claim them. I can remember walking down by Slater's farm. He also had a butcher's shop where Gary Dundas is now. He would slaughter his own pigs and you could often hear them squealing. There were four butchers in Draycott when I was a girl. There was Morgan's, whose shop was opposite Jardine's front entrance, the Co-op had a butchery and there was also Mr Fritchley. Every Christmas he used to hang rabbits and fowls outside and there used to be blood dripping off them. Not nice at all. It's a beauty salon now.

When I was a little girl my dad used to take something called an accumulator down to Mr Orchard, Derek's dad. This would be charged up to make the wireless work. Of course, that row of shops where Orchard's was, in The Market Place, was all the Earl of Harrington's land. The H from the coat of arms of the Harrington family, who lived at Elvaston Castle, can still be seen above the building on the corner of Market Street. A lot of tenants including Mr Beswick, who had the farm and the forge, paid rent to the Harringtons. I can remember going down where Mr Beswick's forge was on South Street and seeing him shoeing horses.

Mrs Savage had a sweetshop in The Market Place and my friend Edna and I used to go in. We weren't allowed make up but when we got to about age 13 we wanted some lipstick so we went to Mrs Savage and asked for 2 oz of liquorish torpedoes, to include 2 red ones. Then we'd go into the telephone box, where there was a little mirror, and put the 'lipstick' on.

The Treetops Hospice shop on Market Street used to be a shop selling pots. Just after the war you couldn't get plates and other types of pots. Harry Lodge had a small lorry with an open back and he used to go up to the Potteries at Stoke buying seconds. Mr Lodge would drive around, tooting the horn or ringing a bell, to let folk know they had pots to sell. The crockery would be packed in straw and Mrs Lodge would sit with it in the back of the lorry to serve you.

Behind the shops, it's The Green now, there used to be some cottages including the one I was born in, number 1 Derby Road.

Mill Yard off Market Street is where Mr Paul first started up during the war, making parts for Spitfires. I think one of my uncles worked there. At one time the mill was used as a firework factory up until the mid-70s.

There used to be several shops in the village in the 40s and 50s. Opposite Jardine's factory there was a little branch of Barclays Bank. There was also Timmy Atkins who sold nails, hammers, creosote, everything like that. There was an overwhelming smell of paraffin because he had a container dispensing it in the shop. No health and safety at that time. A lot of people bought the paraffin because they had the Paul Warmer, manufactured on Longmoor Lane, Breaston. Although the shop seemed in absolute chaos, he always knew exactly what he had in stock. It's now a bridal shop.

Derek Orchard's grandmother used to have a shop selling sewing and knitting goods. It was near where Atkins was on Station Road. I remember us girls, if we were ever trying to make our own clothes, which we did in those days, we'd go and ask Mrs Orchard if we got stuck with it. She would also help us with our knitting. She was lovely, old Grandma Orchard. That's the type of village Draycott was.

Mr and Mrs Smith lived on Nooning Lane and grew vegetables which they sold in their greengrocery shop in the village.

When I was a child, we used to get vans from Long Eaton, coming round selling things. When the Home and Colonial van came the man living opposite my mam used to shout "Are you there Alice? There's the Home and _Conolial_ ."

I remember items which were still rationed after WWII came off ration for the Coronation of Queen Elizabeth. Of course, in those days your mam could make a meal out of nothing. There was a big celebration with trimmed up floats which the kids scrambled on. My cousin Audrey was the Carnival Queen on the float from Fowler Street.

I was always interested in cooking and when I left school, I wanted to go to on a catering course to a college in Derby. However, my mum had other ideas. She told me I was going to work because she had kept me long enough. My dad said nothing, he never did. I was only 15 but she had got me a job at Fletcher's Hosiery, which is now flats in Market Street. I can remember going the day after Boxing day as clear as anything. I walked up some greasy stairs at the back. It had been snowing and I felt completely defeated because it wasn't what I wanted to do. I was to be folding stockings. As I went through the door Miss Bloor greeted me with "Come along and take your coat off and don't keep asking to go to the toilet." She was quite fierce.

When Fletcher's closed, I went to Everlastic at Beeston making bras and things. I really loved it there. After I was married, when I was about 25, my husband Don suggested I should go to Beeston College to study catering. I used to do a lot of cake decorating and I loved doing sugar paste work, especially for weddings.

When my cousin Pat got married her wedding reception had been quite a simple affair as money was short in those days. The cake was an iced sponge, at which one of the bridesmaids had turned her nose up. When it was Pat's golden wedding anniversary, I decided to make her a fruit cake and I decorated it with sugar paste chrysanthemums. Her bouquet had been golden chrysanthemums. I brushed the icing with gold powder, and it looked a treat. When she saw it she was so overcome she burst into tears. It pleased her so much that she showed it off to her family and friends.

Jean Berrisford was a friend of mine. She was very well known in Breaston and had been a teacher and a nurse. She was nursing in India during WWII and met Edwina Mountbatten. Apparently, the nurses were told not to go into the hospital woods at night, in case they bumped into Edwina and Nehru, with whom she was reputed to be having an affair.

When Jean celebrated her 90th birthday she had an open day at her house and asked me if I would make two cakes for her. I was only too happy to do this, and I also helped with serving refreshments on the day.

She remembered I used to talk about Walter Beswick, coming down the lane with Captain to put him in for the night and so, to thank me for helping her, she got an artist friend to paint me a picture. It's nothing like Mr Beswick but it's a man walking down a lane with a horse and it shows the mist, which was often over the canal, in the background. It brings back fond memories.

Jean Berrisford

Sometimes Jean and I would have lunch at Hoggs Bistro. She always had her own table in the window, so she could see what was going on. Jean often wore jodhpurs but when I asked her if she had a horse, she said she hadn't, but she liked wearing the trousers, which were so comfortable.

When she was preparing to go and collect her MBE Jean showed me her hat, which she had bought in a charity shop for £2.50. I said, "You can't go to see the Queen in a hat from a charity shop!" She replied, "I certainly can and afterwards I'm going to take it back and say put £3 on it because it has seen the Queen." Jean died aged 95.

**Our life in Draycott
By Brian Reed
As told to Julia Powell**

Where we started

We came to live in Draycott in 1973 but we had previously rented a hardware shop here before that. When our youngest daughter got to the age of five and started school my wife decided she wanted to go back to work. 23 Victoria Road had become available owing to a family bereavement and the tenant only wanted the money for the stock, he wouldn't ask for anything for the goodwill. Wally Wright, the current Mr Universe at the time, was the owner of the shop and he agreed to us renting it, which we did for about seven years. Wally had a shop next to the old post office and did fruit machines.

When Wally decided to sell the entire property, our accountant advised me to put in an offer. I bought the lot and received the revenue from renting out the four flats. However, Mary my wife's interest was originally in greengrocery and when she saw a greengrocery shop in The Market Place up for sale she asked me if we could buy it. Even though it was a fairly derelict building I decided to buy it on the advice again of my accountant. The owner had only used it for the shop, she didn't live there. It needed a lot doing to it, the toilet was outside and there was no bathroom. Walls were knocked out and central heating was put in and eventually we moved in, having sold my Spondon house to pay for the renovations.

Market Place shops and funfair 1970s

We built up the trade in the shop to such a degree that we took over the contract for supplying greengrocery to the canteen at British Courtaulds Celanese factory. We also supplied the canteen at Ratcliffe Power Station. I would get up early in the morning and go to the market and on the way back drop off the orders at the canteens. A lorry from the market would bring the rest to the shop. Sometimes, when directors or other visitors were expected, we would be asked to supply items which were not generally available. For example strawberries, which at the time could not be bought out of season. These had to

be ordered form Covent Garden in London and would come up as a tray of twelve punnets, but the canteen would only want six. The remainder were sold in the shop and our customers were delighted to have the chance to buy them.
The local nursing home also became one of our customers.

Local shops

Derek Orchard's father used to own the whole row of shops in The Market Place and there used to be a funfair on the land at the end just after Goose Fair. The first shop was a TV and cycle shop. Derek's mother had a sweet shop. We were there with the greengrocer's and next to that was a shoe shop. The one at the end was used by a milkman to store his crates etc. Across the other side of The Market Place was a Co-op. On the main road was a butcher's shop, it is now Bonnie's. The butcher's shop had its own abattoir and one morning as I looked out of my shop window, I saw a cow galloping along on the other side of the road, evidently trying to avoid its demise, with two men in hot pursuit. One of the men shouted to me to shut my door, then the cow ran into the Co-op yard.

Ad for the old Orchard's shop

Where Treetops shop is now used to be a café that Barton's bus drivers could often be seen in. The buses came from Nottingham through Long Eaton and into Draycott but for some reason didn't carry on to Derby.

St Chad's Water

When I first became a parish councillor my responsibilities included looking after what they called the centre of the village, which included the graveyard and St Chad's Water. Well the lake was just a hole in the ground filled with water then. There used to be a large shed in the graveyard that was used during the last war. If any planes came down resulting in crew being killed the bodies were stored there until arrangements could be made for burial.

In the early 1980s the Parish Council bought St Chad's from Hoveringham, part of the Tarmac group, for £1 after they had extracted all the gravel. Before leaving they offered to repair and re surface all the roads in the village, or alternatively landscape around the lake opposite St Chad's Church and put in footpaths trees and plants. The Parish Council decided to take the offer of the landscaping, as they felt the roads were not in too bad a condition. When this was completed St Chad's Water continued to be part of my responsibilities and it was decreed that whilst the general public could walk around there, only the locals would be allowed to fish there. Fishing clubs were created in the six local pubs and the Conservative Club and around forty odd fishermen at a time could often be seen enjoying the facility. Matches took place and eventually ladies' teams were formed. Meetings would be held in one of the pubs to award the winning trophies. The landlord of The Coach and Horses organised a beer barrel rolling and this became part of an open day for the villagers. St Chad's Water is a haven for wildlife and a pleasant place to walk.

Characters

One of the regulars at The Travellers Rest had a dog which he would take for a walk. One morning around ten o'clock he set off with the dog, having been instructed by his wife to be home for lunch at twelve o'clock and to avoid going to the pub. Off they went for the walk but ended up in the pub for a pint. While he was there the man's wife phoned, obviously realising what had happened. The next thing the landlady knew was that a taxi had arrived for her customer. She had just poured him another pint but he told her to hang on to it. Off he went outside with the dog and told the taxi driver to take the dog home, then he returned to finish his pint. *(Ed. I wonder if his lunch was given to the dog.)*

A little girl came into our shop one day, around Christmas time, with her mother's greengrocery order. We were very busy, but she insisted on reading it out rather than passing it to me. All was well until we came to one item whereupon the child stated in a loud voice "My mother wants stuffing". The shop was in uproar, the girl oblivious to the stir she had caused. With as straight a face as I could muster I asked, "Thyme and Parsley or Sage and Onion?"

Factories

The former Draycott Mill lace factory in Market Street has been converted into apartments and small businesses. Opposite a row of houses was probably once occupied by mill workers.

Victoria Mill with its green capped clock tower belonged originally to Thomas Stocks in the 1900s and later merged with Birkin's. It was one of the most important lace factories in the world at one time. Its original tenants were small lace manufacturers who rented a space and a machine from the owner. Ernest Jardine manufactured lace machines. Unbelievably until 1952 there were no inside toilets in the building. By 2004 it was being partially converted into luxury apartments.

Paul's Fabrications had a factory up near Victoria Mill and they used to do work for Rolls Royce.

Did you know?

Draicott (Dry Cote) was mentioned in the Domesday Book in 1086. The people of Wilne gradually moved there as it was on higher ground and not subject to flooding.

Footsteps of Neddytown.
By Janet Galer

I was born in 1955 and lived at Draycott until my mid-20s. Mum was an auxiliary nurse at Draycott Hospital, Hopwell Road and Dad was a toolmaker at Paul's Fabrications. My grandparents lived on Villa Street and an aunty on West Avenue.

I couldn't wait to go to primary school on Hopwell Road, where my teachers were Miss Frith, Miss Haime and Mrs Wooliscroft. I loved learning to read with Janet and John, taking my scruffy pink and grey teddy bear on Friday play afternoons. Mrs Wooliscroft would read stories, *The Magic of the Far Away Tray* being my favourite. She was great doing all the voices and bringing the characters to life.

Our music teacher at junior school was a very glamorous and sophisticated lady, Mrs Woodward who was always exquisitely dressed in broderie suits and matching accessories. I remember singing *The Owl and the Pussycat* and all the hand signals (conducting) and guidance she gave. It gave me a love of singing and music. Mr Elmer played the organ at the church and was my favourite teacher at Western Mere School, Breaston, as he taught my best liked subjects, English and music.

Western Mere School

I lived at the far end of Draycott, just before Breaston, and my friend Marion lived about half way along, so we would often walk the whole length of the village. I loved that there were country walks beyond the houses on either side, without walking too far into the distance. I would pass the Olympic Pub on Station Road, which was re-named for the Tokyo Olympic Games in 1964, and I remember the theme 'Good Morning Tokyo'.

Heatherington's was a fab sweet shop just down the road. They had a penny tray with Love Hearts, Cherry Lips and Palma Violets and jars of goodies, including my favourites, Rhubarb and Custard, Apple Tarts and Pineapple Chunks. It was a proper sweet shop which just sold delicious treats.

Paul's Fabrications gave my dad a concierge job after he suffered a stroke and could no longer do his usual job. They also kept in touch with my mum after my dad died which I think is quite a rare thing nowadays.

Warhurst's was a lovely traditional grocery shop and I remember going there with a list and handing it over at the counter. Years later the current owners were very kind to my mum Linda, and all stood outside out of respect, when it was her funeral, along with other shops along the route.

Over the road two sisters ran the paper shop and I don't even know their first names, always called them the Misses Harris. I loved going there regularly with my dad for my first comic, *Playhour* and sometimes a *Ladybird* book as a treat. Also, the dressing up magazines where you cut out the dresses and put them on a model, later *Lady Penelope* magazine - FAB.

I remember going to my friend's party, she lived next door but one, and all the girls but me were wearing headbands. My mum went to Wilson's Chemist and bought me a lovely hairband with coloured flowers all the way round.

When I was quite young, I used to have my hair cut at Sanderson's barbers. I remember I quite liked the feel of the razor on my neck. Later in my teens my neighbour Janine had a hairdressing salon just up the road and in the 1960s her hair changed colour weekly. She did my hair for a school party once when I was about 13 and made it look lovely, like a really high bouffant. It lasted days and was the best hairstyle I ever had. To me she brought the swinging 60s to a very traditional village. Her dad bred budgerigars and we had our budgie Andy from him. He was a chauffeur to the people who lived at Attewell House and would sometimes give me a lift in the Rolls-Royce Silver Cloud. Every summer there were garden parties at Attewell House and The Lodge on South Street.

We would walk everywhere wearing our casual 'uniform' of quilted anorak and trews. Down Wilne to the river, past the firework factory, Gypsy Lane and back round Hopwell Road. On the cricket field we 'trained' my friend Marion's Jack Russell, Cindy. Over the fields beyond Town End Road my grandpa had a poultry farm. Imagination played a big part in playing and we were always solving mysteries that didn't really exist. That came from reading *The Famous Five* and *Secret Seven* books. It was really exciting. I remember Marion had a zither one Christmas and we used to sing along to it.

As a teenager my paper round covered the whole of Draycott. I had to take three bags on Thursdays because of The Long Eaton Advertiser. I was too small to carry them all or balance them on a bike.

I went to Sunday School at the Methodist Church, Market Street which was a very modern church with a youth club, and also to activities and events in the field behind Mr and Mrs Griffiths house. I saw Mrs Griffiths a couple of years ago and told her that lemon washing up liquid always reminds me of them as their kitchen smelt of it – lovely! I remember singing 'Teddy Bears Picnic' when I was probably about five and later singing in the choir. On the way home, a person pulled up in a car and gave me half a crown, which would perhaps be dodgy nowadays, but it was a genuine gesture.

I have a friend who lives in Draycott now, so I visit quite often. Draycott Hospital is now an upmarket housing development, but a lot remains as it was, and it has retained its old-fashioned values and community spirit. If the shops were as they used to be it would be a great place for visitors. The shops were lovely when I was a girl and it was an idyllic place to grow up. It still is today.

Val Clare's Draycott
As told to Julia Powell

Draycott is often nicknamed Neddytown by the locals. There have been several explanations for this, but it is most probably because coal carts were originally pulled by donkeys from the north and Draycott was a changing point, somewhere near the Co-op cottages, before Derby Canal took over the trade.

My husband and I first came to live in Draycott around 1978. It was only supposed to be a temporary move, but I still live in the same house today. We needed a four bedroomed house, because we both had children from previous marriages and there weren't many large houses around at the time.

The first day we moved in we hadn't got a TV aerial, so my husband went into Derek Orchard's shop in the village to buy a portable one. Derek was an electrician and sold electrical goods, but his main trade was in bicycles.

He said we wouldn't get a signal in Draycott, but my husband told him we were right on the edge of the village. Derek was dubious but agreed to lend us an aerial. Sadly, we didn't get a signal so back it went. However, within a couple of days we had arranged for one to be put up and duly received a signal.

Because we had a business in Derby, we tended to shop around the market there but locally we used Wilson's the chemist, the newsagent and occasionally the chip shop, which still remains on the main road.

I became quite quickly involved with the Borough Council because I had only just lost my seat in the city of Derby. Because my husband was abroad a lot, I joined the local Conservatives and, with time on my hands, I wanted to get involved with the local community. June Parkinson sent one of the local parish councillors to see me. He turned out to be my next-door neighbour and before long, I too became a member of the parish council and I still am. This was early 1980s.

Mary Burrows was the parish clerk when I joined the Draycott Parish Council, she knew everyone in the village and was a great source of knowledge. Val Lewis took over from Mary when she retired and managed to obtain funds to rebuild the pavilion on the cricket ground on Hopwell Road and the parish rooms on Elvaston Street that we use nowadays. She retired recently.

In the early 1980s Draycott Parish Council purchased some land, including the lake at St Chads from Tarmac for £1. We then had to decide what we were going to do with it and decided to make it into a nature reserve. People seemed generally happy with what has happened down there. We've spent quite a lot of money on it and worked with advisors to remove non-native trees. The lake itself was a problem to us at first, because we envisaged canoeing and other water sports, but then we realised that it is exceedingly deep. Also, a lot of weed grows in it, which makes it very dangerous, both for swimming and other water sports. Eventually we decided that the only safe thing to do was to restrict it to fishing. There is a covenant imposed by Tarmac which doesn't allow any non-residents of Draycott to fish the water. Therefore, it cannot become a commercial fishing club. Basically, the gift of the lake to the residents for £1 was by way of recompense for all the years of inconvenience caused by the removal of gravel. The public are free to walk around but not fish in the lake.

Six weeks after I moved to the village I was asked if I would be a school governor at Draycott Primary, later Draycott Community Primary School. I took that up and continued until 2016. All my children were pupils there. I remember a charity fund raiser we once did when we wanted to draw attention to the plight of children in Africa, who had to walk miles to obtain clean water. Half of the governors walked to ASDA in Long Eaton to collect a gallon of water and carried it back to Draycott. Later we had a reception and buffet at the school.

Draycott Primary School

Two of my children went on to Western Mere Secondary School. Sadly, the school was closed in 1990 and pulled down in 1992 after my son left. It was a shame really as it had a lovely lecture theatre where school productions took place, but maybe it was getting a bit tired.

When I came to the village Jardine's was used for the manufacture of small electronic items, industrial grills and things for the catering industry. I believe sections were rented out to various businesses. Eventually part of the mill was turned into flats.

One of the big things that changed Draycott was when Adrian Perkins and Gary Dundas decided something needed to be done to brighten up the village. They founded the Draycott Village Fund in 2012 and came up with the idea of having Christmas trees mounted on brackets above the shops, along the main road. Flags are also mounted for certain occasions. Money was raised for other improvements to be made and some residents soon asked if they could have the Christmas trees and flags on their house frontages. There were well over 200 trees in the village in 2017.

My grandfather, Herbert Selwood
By Keith Reedman

About 1900 Herbert Selwood, my grandfather, came to Long Eaton as an economic migrant. He was born in 1882 in a remote hamlet called Inglestone Common on the Gloucestershire-Somerset border. Here he grew up as the eldest of a family of eleven children and became an agricultural worker after leaving school in Wickwar. One or two of his mother's family had left the district and settled in Long Eaton, which at the turn of the century was a rapidly expanding lace manufacturing town, where there were many employment opportunities. Word of these opportunities reached back to the Selwood family and my grandfather decided to try his luck.

After arriving in Long Eaton, Herbert soon found employment as a drayman, having had several years' experience with horses. His first job as a carter was in making deliveries of lace from the lace factories in Long Eaton to the Lace Market in Nottingham, where the 'brown' lace was finished. Although there was a direct railway connection, lace was always transported by road to Nottingham where it then became Nottingham lace.

Within a few years the whole family moved to Long Eaton and settled in Acton Road. Herbert met and married my grandmother but before long he was beset by health problems. He was advised to take an indoor job and for a few years worked in Beeston Maltings. He and his young family moved to Windsor Street and it was there that my mother was born in 1909. For whatever reason Herbert's health did not improve, so he returned to Long Eaton and obtained a job with the Co-operative Society as a bread delivery man, using a horse-drawn bread van.

This is what my grandfather did from my earliest memory of him. Early each morning he would collect his horse from the stables in Chapel Street and walk it through the town, on the right-hand side of the road (facing the traffic), to the bakery in Fletcher Street, where his van had been loaded up ready. He then hitched his horse and went on his round.

Co-op bread van

One day, probably in the school holidays in 1944, I went with him, riding by his side, quite high up. We went to Risley and Hopwell, down Gypsy Lane to the houses by the canal bridge and back through Draycott and Breaston. I do not remember having anything to eat on the trip, but I do recall the big strong horse having his nose bag of oats.

When I was quite young, I was allowed to rummage in my grandfather's tool drawer at his Sandford Avenue house (I still proudly own and use some of his tools). In the bottom of the drawer was a collection of small steel objects, which had a chisel edge. These interested me but at the time I did not think to ask their purpose. They were studs which were inserted into the holes in a horse shoe so that the horse could get a grip on snow and ice.

Sadly, my grandfather died in 1946, the result of suffering from stomach ulcers for much of his working life. Luckily for us now, this condition is no longer fatal.

Co-op wheelwright's shop, Chapel Street

Long Eaton Weight Lifting Club.
By Lyndsey Fairbrother

My father, Thomas James Fairbrother, founded the Long Eaton Weightlifting Club in 1930. It was located between Hawthorne Avenue and Derwent Street. There were some early connections with Russell Street Gym, with members using both facilities. Tom ran the Club from 1930 until his death in September 1973.

Photograph 1946

During WWII my father was away for 5 years, serving in a Royal Artillery Regiment. However, my grandfather kept the Club ticking over in his absence.

Greg Fairbrother, Tom's youngest son, continued to run the club with the assistance of Brian Heyhoe until 1976, when the land was sold to Clutsom & Kemp. Then the Club continued at Community House on Derby Road until its final closure in 1992.

Tom won many competitions and championships and set many records as his collection of medals and cups testify to. He won the British Heavyweight Weightlifting Championship in 1935 and anticipated competing in the 1936 Berlin Olympics. Unfortunately, at the Olympic trials in early 1936, he failed to complete his lifts. Apparently, he had a 'bit of previous history' with that particular referee, but he never used it as an excuse.

However, Tom and several Club members, wives and girlfriends had been saving for the trip since 1932 so they decided to go anyway. They went to Barton's Bus Depot and hired a coach and driver, then they bought a map of Europe and prepared to journey to the Berlin Olympics. This was an amazing thing to do in those times!

I remember my mother telling me, in later years, that at the opening ceremony Hitler and Goering were driven around the stadium in an open car, with the Nazi crowd Zeig Heiling at full volume. When they passed the tiny Long Eaton contingent they were greeted with a chorus of 'raspberries'! I think they were lucky to survive the encounter.

An interesting adjunct to this was that during the last war Tom's regiment occupied some German office buildings that had very recently been vacated by the retreating German army. He picked up a document with the German eagle motif in gold lettering, which contained Hitler's signature. My guess is that he reflected on seeing Hitler at the Olympics and now he had his autograph.

Ed

In addition to Lyndsey's story there are several other interesting anecdotes about Tom Fairbrother. The following are just a few of them: -

Aged 18 he walked to Derby to try lifting a special long handled hammer, something which had evidently defeated all previous contenders. He succeeded and was awarded his first medal by the astonished blacksmith.

On another occasion Thomas Inch, a professional strongman, placed the sum of £15 on a dumb bell and challenged anyone to lift it. Tom lifted it above his head with one hand and won himself the prize of a motorcycle.

Extolling the virtues of Hovis as a muscle builder and stamina giver, Tom's letter and photograph appeared, alongside those of other champion athletes and bodybuilders, in a health magazine ad for Hovis.

Clifford Charles Page attended the Long Eaton club and remembers Tom won the Great Britain Body Building title and appeared in the Health and Efficiency magazine. Cliff recalls Tom was a lovely man, a gentle giant with whom he worked at Gimson and Slaters the upholsterers.

Gary John Reed attended the club when it moved to Derby Road. He still has his membership card.

Gary's membership card

Long Eaton Memories 1963 – 1972.
By Susan Halesworth

We moved to Briar Gate in Long Eaton from the then sleepy village of Castle Donington in October of 1963. I believe it was Election Day 15th October 1963, when Alec Douglas Home's government lost and Harold Wilson's premiership commenced. I was six years old, my brother Russell three. Until we moved away from Long Eaton in 1972 my father, Brian Halesworth, worked in power stations along 'Megawatt Valley' (the power generating industry's nickname for the Trent Valley, as there were so many power stations on the river). Amongst them there was one in Castle Donington and one in Spondon, the latter being unique in that it supplied power directly to British Celanese next door. I suspect most people in the area remember the smell which emanated from British Celanese, often pervading the area when the wind was in the right direction. By 2017 only Ratcliffe-on-Soar, Cottam and West Burton remained in service of the coal-fired power stations in 'Megawatt Valley'.

Wellington Street Infants School

I joined Wellington Street Infants School for the remainder of the academic year before moving up to Highfields in the summer of 1964. My first friend at this school was Megan Reeve, whose family lived on Breedon Street. I am happy to report that we have continued our friendship over the years and, although we now live in different countries, we still stay in touch and see each other as often as we can.

Each day I made the 20-minute journey to and from school on foot, walking along Canal Street, turning into William Street, crossing College Street into Cavendish Road, through the school gates into the playground – only concrete in those days. The names of the teachers I recall were Class Two, Mrs Cooke, Class Three Mrs McDermott and in Class Four Miss Poxon. I have a feeling that Miss Poxon also took us in Class One which is maybe why I don't remember another teacher's name. Miss Cordingly was Head Mistress.

There were a number of playground games – the usual ones: skipping, cat's cradle, hopscotch and some more which are probably not terribly PC these days. The one that particularly stands out in my memory is Japs and Commandos! The whole school population would split into two groups and 'adopt' a home territory at opposite ends of the playground. There would be a charge and a grabbing of opponents, in an attempt to drag them to your home territory as POWs! Whichever team had captured the most prisoners, by the time the bell rang for the end of playtime, were the winners. I don't think we would have even known who the Japs and Commandos were if we had been asked! We also acted out scenes from our favourite films. *The Sound of Music* was a particular favourite, being the blockbuster that it was.

As regularly as Christmas came around, so did the school Nativity play. There were only four classes, and each would be assigned different roles each year. Competition for the leading roles of Mary and Joseph was particularly fierce. It was always the same story, nothing 'untraditional' for Highfields. One year our class were the sheep and the shepherds, and we all had to crawl around on all fours wrapped in a white bed-sheet. One girl, playing a shepherd, was on stage walking around in bare feet and stood on a drawing pin, which must have hurt. However, she had a speaking part and carried on regardless. Mrs McDermott, our teacher, held her up as an example for all to follow. Carry on regardless!

We celebrated other Church festivals and a particular memory is Harvest Festival each autumn. We all had to contribute an item of food to demonstrate the bounty of the harvest. I believe the food was donated to an old folks home after we had held the assembly. The School Hymnal had been handed to us at the beginning of our sojourn at Highfields and we were allowed to keep it on leaving the school. I still have mine. We also had a day out at Wades on Wellington Street each year, touring the factory to see and hear about upholstered furniture assembly. We walked from the school in a crocodile line, two by two, led by and rear guarded by teachers. I don't recall knowing that Long Eaton was an important centre for the manufacture of sofas at the time. Of course, that is still true nowadays.

My grandfather James Frayne
By Margaret Jennings

James was born in County Mayo in 1883 and moved to Cobden Street, Long Eaton to work for his uncle Jimmy Frayne, who was a plasterer. Jimmy was fond of betting. In 1904 my grandfather married Maggie Duffy in Kilmore and moved to Sawley shortly afterwards, where John Patrick was born in 1905, Honoria Mary 1906, (my mother) James Lawrence 1909 and lastly Dominic. They lived on Wilsthorpe Road and then moved to a fine house called Carmel on Hawthorne Avenue, where they remained until my grandfather's death in 1962. The garden of Grandad Frayne's house was huge and used to extend to Myrtle Avenue. He also used to own premises on Tamworth Road near The Royal Oak, where he had an underground storage facility. Petrol stored in there was used during the Suez crisis. My sister was able to use some of this in order to go on honeymoon.

Grandpa (on Grandma's right) and Grandma in a line up

Grandad worked for Perks plastering business but later started his own firm. His lorries were inscribed *'For everything in plastering the Fraynes of Long Eaton are the people'*. James had a gentle Irish brogue and would lapse into Gaelic if he didn't want his children to know what he was saying. He was a staunch Catholic and used to wear a little emblem to show he didn't drink alcohol. The family attended St Francis of Assisi on Tamworth Road and they all married from that church. The children attended the local primary school. Mum's brothers went to Long Eaton Grammar School and she went to St Catherine's in Nottingham.

James was the first Catholic to be elected Chairman of the Long Eaton Urban District Council, something which made him very proud.

Grandfather died in 1962, predeceased by my grandmother and they are both buried in Long Eaton Cemetery.

Jimmy Frayne as recalled by Keith Reedman

Firstly, I cannot with certainty say that I knew him, but I do know that his firm did more or less all the plastering for the houses and other buildings built by my father. I can visualise him, but this might be because I can recognise him in a photo.

His plasterer's yard was on Tamworth Road in Long Eaton nearer to the canal bridge from the site of the Royal Oak. Until recently redeveloped, there was a filling station owned originally by Tom Oakley. The plasterer's yard went from Tamworth Road up to the canal and always looked a mess. Plastering is a messy business and in the 1920s and 30s plasterers made their own plaster from raw materials.

LONG EATON'S CHIEF CITIZEN

COUNCILLOR JAMES FRAYNE, J.P.

The dignity of a township is crystallised in the position of chief citizen, and where communal traditions are not lightly observed, the honours of occupancy are only accorded those who by sincerity and continuity of service have "won their spurs."

It is fitting that 39 years' residence in Long Eaton on the part of Councillor J. Frayne, J.P., has been crowned by his election to the chairmanship of the Long Eaton Urban District Council, following a year in the vice-chair. This apportionment —which was confirmed at the annual meeting of the Council on April 29 —to the record of Councillor Frayne of the honour of chief citizenship is deserved by reason of many years of loyal and conscientious service given without thought of personal gain or individual aggrandizement.

An Irishman by birth and tradition, Councillor Frayne migrated to Long Eaton in 1894 and received his education at the Long Eaton National Schools—upon leaving which he entered upon an apprenticeship as a plasterer. Persistence and ability have so been applied to his industrial labours by Councillor Frayne that to-day he is well-established as a master-plasterer.

Elected in 1924 to share in the representation of the New Sawley Ward on the Long Eaton Council, Mr. Frayne has passed through the chair of the Public Health Committee and also has sat on the committees of Highways, Electricity, Water, Ambulance and Fire Brigade, Markets, Finance, and Free Library, of the latter of which he was at one period vice-chairman.

An ardent Roman Catholic, Councillor Frayne has made many friends by his broad-mindedness and practical sympathy, and his year as chairman should be one in which the fellowship of the Council will develop and the progress of business be subjected to thoughtful control.

Mills Dockyard, Trent Lock, Sawley
By Steve Mills.
As told to Julia Powell.

The Dockyard

The boatyard has been in my family since the late 1800s. My great grandfather, Amos Mills worked as a wheelwright on the site of Oakley's Garage which was on Tamworth Road, backing on to the canal. I guess he was dabbling in wheelwrighting and boats and in fact anything made of wood. I think he came and took over

Mills Dockyard today

the yard in the late 1800s and the family has been here ever since. Amos Mills was building and repairing barges for carrying cargo and he was also building houseboats for Trent Lock and further down the River Trent. He built rowing skiffs in the two-storey building which is still here. The Rice family used to hire these skiffs out at Trent Lock.

There was apparently quite a lot of traffic up and down the canal at one time, but it went into decline after WW2. In the late 40s and the 50s and 60s there wasn't a pleasure boat industry as such. My grandfather Cyril Mills came into the business after leaving the army. He was a very clever engineer and used to do marine engine conversions for old clinker lifeboats, which were brought onto the canal. The leisure boat industry as we know it now didn't really exist then.

There has always been a houseboat community hereabouts, six to eight boats maximum, but not many people used to live on boats, certainly not to the extent that they do now. It's an accepted lifestyle at all the marinas nowadays, made popular by TV series etc.

I've come across several characters over the years. One was Ike Argent, an old boatman who came from a family of boatmen. His daughter still rents a workshop from me for doing boat covers and hoods. Ike was one of the most knowledgeable canal people there ever was. He travelled extensively and worked for the British Waterways Board.

I came into the boatyard business in the late 1970s. I was an apprentice at Rolls Royce working on aero engines, but I didn't care for being just a number in a factory all day long. Thereafter I went through a variety of jobs including a roofing contractor and a landscape gardener, because that got me outside. Then I started doing bits and bobs in the boatyard but there still wasn't any real leisure boat industry, although it was beginning to go that way. People wanted work doing on their boats, so I used to black them up for a bit of pocket money. My father didn't work in the business, he was a college lecturer, so he just ran it part time with the moorings. Around 1980 I took the business over full time and in those days, I used to get by rebuilding wooden boats. There were a lot of old ex admiralty boats on the canals, old clinker lifeboats, Broads boats from Norfolk, which were always wooden built. They were always leaking and there was nobody really doing those sorts of repairs, so it got me into the business and I just went from there. I became a wooden boat builder and restorer for up to the late 1990s. I've restored some beautiful wooden boats including racing boats, hydroplanes and steam launches. As the leisure industry grew to the sort we have now that kept the dry dock busy and I drifted into that and the two went hand in hand and that's where I am right up to the present. The large dry dock is rented out to people on a weekly basis from a Saturday morning to the following Saturday morning, when people can do their own painting and repairs, or they can hire us to do that for them. It's generally for narrow boat work but we also do Dutch barges. Folks come up from Newark, Lincoln and further afield.

Houseboats at Trent Lock today

I took over my houseboat from my grandmother after she died. It had been on site since the early 1920s but it was only a single storey 45-foot boat. I was fortunate enough to have three daughters, so as the family grew the boat had to grow. We went from 45 to 65 feet and then I made it into a two-storey boat. It was re-bottomed with a wooden bottom in the 1930s and we think the metal framed windows were put in then. When I put the top storey on it, I went to a glazing firm in Long Eaton and salvaged some metal window frames from their skip, which looked exactly the same, so I bought them and incorporated them in the rebuild. It looks original. I made all the brackets and railings etc and gave it a period feel. Folk think it's a Mississippi River boat.

My grandfather's bungalow, now occupied by my brother and his family, has been here since the late 1800s and the bungalow where my parents lived, and I grew up, is still here. We've never wandered far.

Around and about

The Trent Lock Golf course is on both sides of Lock Lane but on the left-hand side of the lane there used to be a railway tip which was filled in with ash from Toton steam engines.

Prior to that it was a lake where my father used to go sailing. It's where the Trent Valley Sailing Club started many years ago

Holes can still be seen in the fields where bombs were dropped from wartime aircraft aiming for the railway bridge. There was one dropped in the farmer's field behind the Steamboat Inn and I gather the lock cottage opposite the pub received a direct hit and was flattened.

The Trent Lock Inn was originally called the Trent Navigation and that pub and The Steamboat Inn have been around for years. The Steamboat was one of the first pubs in the area to be themed. Because the landlord was an ex sub mariner he decorated it with nautical artefacts and made it quite a popular pub in his time.

Terry who runs The Lock House Tea Room is also a sign writer for the boats.

Memories of Sawley
By Joan Rippengal (née Reedman)

The house where I was born was built in 1932 in what was then an unmade road called Gladstone Street, but after Long Eaton 'took over' Sawley it became Northfield Avenue, because Long Eaton already had a Gladstone Street. Northfield Avenue was then mainly surrounded by fields and remained unmade until 1958, when it was given a tarmac surface (my father had to pay for our frontage) to join up with the new Townside estate roads. Before then there was just a rough track to the end of Shaftesbury Avenue.

My mother bought a lot of small holly plants – I remember they were 7s. 6d. (37½p) a dozen – and planted them at the bottom of the back garden, hoping that eventually they would deter the horses and cattle in Grammer's Farm field from leaning over the fence and grazing the plants in our garden. By the time the hollies were big enough to do that the field had gone and a row of old peoples' bungalows, on the big post-war council housing estate, had been built there. Until this was built Draycott Road ended by The Manse (no. 22) with an iron kissing gate and a path over the field, which led to another kissing gate and stile by a pond and the bus stop on the main road. In those days it was the A453 Nottingham to Birmingham road, via Tamworth, hence its name, Tamworth Road. On the opposite side of the road was a little triangle with elm trees at the end of Lock Lane. Dr Highfield often stopped there, presumably to have his lunch sandwiches, before coming to visit me after I had been very ill. We could spot his little car from a bedroom window. During the war the bus stop was removed, like many others, to conserve fuel, so we had to go either to the Nag's Head in Old Sawley, or the Bell Hotel in New Sawley.

Shopping

We did our Sawley shopping – as opposed to Long Eaton shopping – almost exclusively at Bexon's on the corner of Draycott Road and Towle Street. Bexon's had its own bakery and also sold general groceries and Lyon's Maid Ice Cream. Across the road, on the corner of Grosvenor Avenue, was Humphrey's, also bakers and grocers. They sold Wall's Ice Cream, but we seldom went there, and we considered Bexon's bread and Lyon's ice cream to be quite definitely superior! We usually bought ice cream cornets, a cone shaped wafer with a cylinder of ice cream, either vanilla or half and half - vanilla and strawberry. These cylinders were wrapped in two strips of overlapping cream paper. When you pulled each side the ice cream dropped into the cone. Very neat. Occasionally an ice cream boy would come along Tamworth Road, laboriously pedalling on his tricycle. In front was a heavy insulated chest on two wheels and the lad sat on the saddle with the rear wheel behind. This ice cream was 'loose' and was scooped out for cornets (1d. or 2d.). To make a 'wafer' he had an aluminium device on a handle into which he would put a rectangular wafer. He then adjusted the depth of the base by a notch on the handle – higher up for a threepenny one, lower for a sixpenny one – and paddled the ice cream in and levelled it off. On went the second wafer and the notch was moved to the top position which pushed the whole thing out. Ice cream was banned after the outbreak of war.

Our milk was originally delivered to the back door by Dorothy Camp, who came around in her little pony and trap. There were usually two full sized churns in the trap and a smaller one which she carried to the door. This had two long-handled dippers hooked over the rim, one each for measuring a pint and a half-pint, and she ladled the milk into the family's milk jug. After the Camps gave up their milk round we had it delivered in glass bottles from Hutchings in Long Eaton.

Old Sawley didn't have many shops. Besides Bexon's and Humphrey's there was the excellent chip shop in Arnold Avenue, opposite the Womens' Institute hall; Barker's the newsagent and barber, a fairly modern building in a rather unlikely position on the outside corner of Firs Street and Arnold Avenue and Wright's the shoe shop in Plant Lane. Rooke's was the Post Office, General Stores and Off-Licence opposite the Nag's Head, the Co-op was next to Bothe Hall on the Harrington Arms side of Tamworth Road and Cowley's grocery shop was on the corner of Tamworth Road and East End.

New Sawley had a greater range of shops, most of them on the east side of Tamworth Road between Hey Street and Roosevelt Avenue. There was also a garage near Roosevelt Avenue, where petrol was laboriously pumped by hand to fill vehicles. The New Sawley Co-op was bigger and more modern than Old Sawley's. I remember the wartime posters on the walls in the greengrocery section, promoting 'Potato Pete' and 'Doctor Carrot'. There was a wonderful aerial system for payment. The counter assistant wrote out the total cost and your dividend number in duplicate on a pad using carbon paper and tore off the tickets. He put these into a little tub with your money, screwed the tub into a holder and pulled a handle which shot the tub up to the cashier sitting high up in a glass-fronted cabin. She then retained one ticket and shot the other back along with your change. Co-op dividends were paid out at regular intervals.

This shop was on our way home from Infant School and sometimes during the war there would be a queue outside. We always asked what had 'come in', and if it was something on blue ration books (for children between 5 and 14) such as oranges, we would race home for the books and some cash and dash back hoping they hadn't sold out.

A huge Indian pedlar, wearing a turban and carrying an enormous suitcase of cotton goods, used to call at the back door every year and it was amazing how much was crammed into that case. One year a large tufted cotton rug was bought for my bedroom. Apart from Dr Denny this was the only non-white person we ever saw until the American troops came during the war.

Residents.

I remember being amused that there were families called Salt and Pepper in the village, though sadly they did not live next door to each other. Most of the people I knew lived along Draycott Road. The Walkers and later Jarmans in The Manse, Tiveys, Brooks (Dorothy Brooks had a bull terrier which I didn't like), Browns, Wilmotts and Wagners. I played quite a lot with Pat Wagner whose family lived next door to the three Misses Brown on Draycott Road, between Clarke Drive and Grosvenor Avenue. Pat's father was an AA patrol man, resplendent in uniform and gauntlets on his yellow motorbike with sidecar. He always saluted drivers who had an AA badge on their car (unless there was a speed trap). One day during the war when I was at their house, I mentioned that my mother had some records of music by Wagner, but she said it was pronounced 'Varg-ner', and they pronounced their name 'Wag-ner'. I said I thought it was funny that the names were the same, but they pronounced theirs differently There was a very awkward silence and I didn't understand why. It hadn't dawned on me that the composer was German, as Pat's family must have been originally, and in wartime they were naturally very sensitive on the subject.

I have two memories of people being upset by wild flowers I had picked in innocence. One occasion was when we children filled and decorated frail baskets for our contribution to Harvest Festival at Sawley Baptist Chapel. I went down Wilne Lane and found a most unusual plant climbing in the hedge. I picked it and wound it round the handle of my basket, but it was strongly disapproved of by one member of the congregation. This was because it was a wild hop and hops were used for brewing and he was, like the great majority, if not all of the congregation, a staunch teetotaller.

I used to visit Miss Elsie Bowmer at Corner Croft along Draycott Road. She was an invalid and used a wheelchair but had a great interest in the outside world, particularly the natural world. I tried to take something interesting to show or give her every time I went. It might be a flower or just a sea shell or pretty stone, if I'd been away, and she had a special little border in the sun-trap outside the back door where she put such things. One day the May blossom seemed especially lovely and I cut a few sprays to take to her but was astonished when Emily, the maid, answered the door and would not let me in. She believed the May blossom was unlucky and meant death. I'm sure Miss Bowmer, who was well educated, would not have had the same views, but I was banned that day. Emily's speciality as a cook was caraway seed cake and on happier visits, I was sometimes allowed a slice.

The Bowmer family was prominent in the village. Mr Joe Bowmer, Elsie's father, had been the farmer at Sawley Grange, on the way to Draycott along Draycott Lane. He was a fine, tall, upright figure and probably bought Corner Croft on his retirement. He was the first person I remember achieving the astonishing age of 80! During the War he would sometimes call at our house and my mother, who didn't like cheese, would give him her ration, paltry as it was. As she remarked, when he was farming, he probably ate that amount in one mouthful. I do remember how grateful he was. A younger brother, Frank later came to live with his wife and daughter Susan at The Haven, on the corner of Draycott Road and Firs Street. My brother and I had often visited Mr and Mrs Russell, who lived there before. Mr Russell had an aviary in the garden, with lots of colourful budgerigars. They also had a Scottie dog and a shallow ornamental pond with a concrete plaque like a little gravestone at one end, inscribed with the cliché verse:

'The kiss of the sun for pardon, the song of the birds for mirth,

One is nearer God's heart in a garden than anywhere else on earth'

Mikado Road Infants' School.

Unlike many people I have no recollection of my first day at school, nor do I know when I started. As my 5th birthday was in April 1940 I may have gone in September 1939, or in the spring or summer of 1940. Whenever it was, it was wartime. My brother is about two years older than me and after the first one or two days when Mother escorted us there and back I just went along with him. Strictly speaking we lived in the Old Sawley School catchment area, but Mikado Road Infants had a better reputation. It was certainly a more modern school, sadly now closed.

The first thing I clearly remember was the milk régime. On Monday mornings we had to put tuppence ha'penny on our desks. Milk came in one third of a pint bottles which cost

Mikado Road School

one halfpenny each, so I soon learned that five halves make two and a half. There was a fuss if someone had forgotten their milk money or didn't bring the right amount. Before morning playtime, we put our milk mat on the desk in front of us and the milk monitor put the bottle on it, so that there was no mess on the table top. When we first arrived at school we were all given a piece of thick material, about four inches square, with instructions to embroider it to make it personal and distinctive. Losing one's milk mat was serious.

In those days milk bottles had a wide top with a cardboard disc seal. The disc was partially punched with a finger-sized circle. The theory was that when you pressed it, your finger broke the seal and there was a neat hole for the straw to go through. In practice this did not always happen. Very often the hole was insufficiently punched and the harder you pushed the more likely it was that the whole top would collapse into the bottle, with the inevitable splash and spillage. Hence the milk mats. The cardboard discs often had a further life. If the holes were nicely central, two were put together with the centres removed and wool scraps were wrapped round and round, from the hole to the outer edge and back through the hole until the centre was completely filled. Then the wool was carefully cut through at the edge, between the two discs and another length of wool was tightly wound and knotted between them. Then the discs were removed, and the resulting pom-pom was rounded off. Two or three pom-poms were often hung on the hood of a pram to keep the baby amused.

The crates of milk were delivered early and stood outside until morning playtime. In hot weather this meant that the milk was warm. Sometimes it was 'off'. We had some extremely cold winters in the 1940s and I remember days when the milk froze in the bottles. The expansion caused the frozen cream on the milk to rise up like a soufflé and push the tops off. It was quite exciting, but not as good as ice cream.

At first when I was at Mikado Road School the straws were real straws – that is, they were made of wheat or other cereal stalks - and they are things I remember with tremendous pleasure. They were a glorious colour, they made a lovely sound in the box, they were light and strong and they worked! They came in boxes of 144 and we were taught that that was a gross, twelve twelves, or a dozen dozens. Sadly, the supply of these straws stopped. I expect they had come from the continent, or else the straw was needed in wartime for other purposes. The replacements were pathetic and caused endless problems. They were made of strips of slightly waxed, pale straw-coloured paper, spiralled round and very poorly gummed. Soon after they were introduced to the milk they started to come unwound at the bottom and the top flattened when you began to suck. Then you had to try to squeeze them open again or tear the top off and try again. Many of us, although we didn't have refrigerators at home in those days, found lukewarm milk hard to stomach, especially if it had begun to 'turn'. But milk had to be drunk and there was no going out for playtime until it was. And no playtime meant no opportunity to 'cross the yard', the euphemism for going to the WCs. Those warm milk days were a torment.

There was a series of number-teaching posters on the walls round the classroom. At the top was the appropriate number of big shiny coloured paper spots arranged like domino dots, with a different colour for each number (five was green) and underneath was the figure, very large. There were also posters showing weights and measures. In the cupboard were tins of brightly coloured wooden beads and laces for threading. I don't know whether these were to help with number work or just manual dexterity. We wrote in chalk on individual blackboards of compressed cardboard with a black finish. These blackboards lived in a pocket hung on the back of our chairs. The pockets were made of a thick material, probably crash, and I remember making mine at home, with my mother's help. The material was the width of the chair back, plus turnings, and was folded over and sewn at the sides for about 4 or 5 inches. This part fitted over the back of the chair. The long piece then went down the back outside for the length of the blackboard and was turned back up for about 8 inches and those edges stitched together. But before that was done you had to embroider the part of the back which would show. I chose an outline picture of a whale from my mother's box of transfer patterns and embroidered the whale in salmon pink chain stitch. It seems extraordinary now that 5-year olds were expected to embroider but of course in those days their mothers all knew how. In school it came under the heading of Handwork.

Our 'Readers' were the Mack and Tosh primers, all about two Scottie dogs, one black, one white. I don't remember learning to read – it just seemed to happen.

In the school hall was a very big dolls' house on a stand. I can't imagine what its teaching purpose was, and its door was only opened on special occasions. My mother made a canvas runner embroidered in tent stitch for its hallway. It would have been over a foot long. Also, in the school hall were piles of oval mats made of sisal. We used to take a mat after dinnertime, spread it on the floor and lie down and we were expected to sleep for a while. I imagine this afternoon rest was just for the 'babies', the reception class. A less peaceful occupation in the hall was percussion music. There was a collection of instruments - drums, tambourines, triangles, bells on wooden rods, castanets and cymbals - which were beaten, struck, shaken or clashed in time to the music played on the piano. I always seemed to get a castanet or a triangle, but I longed to play the drum, which was the obvious favourite with the boys. I can remember having some BBC wireless lessons of *Music and Movement with Ann Driver*. They were wonderful.

Miss Jones, who lived in Breaston, was the Headmistress and her office was in the middle of the building. After the outbreak of war there was a big diphtheria immunisation programme for schoolchildren. Our mothers came and we queued at Miss Jones' desk while the nurse checked the list and inoculated us with a huge blunt needle. The boys cried most.

The other teachers I remember were rotund Miss Turner, who lived in Hey Street and Miss Powdrill who lived in Shaftesbury Avenue. One day the weather turned wet and Miss Powdrill kept us in school until she said there was enough blue in the sky to make a sailor a pair of trousers. I had never heard that expression before, but I still use it. She would have been mindful of the difficulties mothers had in drying clothes in wet weather, and would not have taken it for granted that a change of clothes would be available in every home. After I nearly died of meningitis in March 1943 Miss Powdrill gave me a delightful, illustrated story book for my 8th birthday. I still love it and often used it when I was teaching. My other book which is connected with Mikado Road School is a copy of *The Water Babies* which was 'Presented by the Trustees of the Sawley Charities'. Sadly it is not dated but I know it was regarded as a prize for good work.

On the Turner Road side of the school grounds was a grassy area and we were told that this measured half an acre; since then I have always had a good idea of what half an acre looks like. The school's air raid shelters were built in one part of this green and we spent many hours down there. I don't remember what we did, but I expect that teaching continued and there were certainly story times. We always lived in hope that Mr Tucker, to us a very old gentleman who lived nearby in Bradshaw Street near the Monkey Park, would arrive as he sometimes did, and give out new pennies or ha'pennies to the children. (Something to give modern sociologists a heart attack!)

One highlight of my time at Mikado Road was the visit of the famous New Zealand airwoman Miss Jean Batten, who came to receive the money which had been collected for the Anglo-French Ambulance Corps. I was chosen to present the purse to her and had to practise my curtsey. Miss Jones made sure that I would be wearing a white dress which Mother had made for me; the whole bodice, front and back, was elaborately smocked in rows of pastel coloured embroidery. It certainly was a special dress and Miss Jones obviously thought it would make the right impression in front of the bigwigs – and a photographer from the Long Eaton Advertiser might be there!

Despite wartime, school photographs were still taken of all the children individually or with their siblings. There is one of my brother and me side by side, taken in what was then my classroom. We both looked a bit scruffy and I still had a big scar on my knee following an impetigo infection. Next year's school photograph was of me alone, Keith having gone on to Tamworth Road School, and I was wearing the famous smocked dress.

Something which people nowadays would find amazing was that, in a state school, at the age of six, we learned psalms by heart – but they were the Prayer Book version, not from the Authorised Bible. The first one I remember learning was Psalm 8 – '*O Lord our Governor, how excellent is Thy name in all the world*'. I liked the versions we were taught, and innocently asked at home for a Prayer Book of my own. That really set the cat among the pigeons, as my family were strictly non-conformist Baptist. To my parents' great credit I did get a Prayer Book, but also a Bible, on my seventh birthday. Both books were illustrated, the Bible with Old Masters, and I treasured them. It is hard to realise how firmly the battle lines were drawn then between different denominations, chapel and church. My mother, who wouldn't have anything to do with Sawley Parish Church or the Church of England in general, was really indignant when the Rector of Sawley sent his daughters to the Roman Catholic Convent School in Long Eaton. And yet, when I was at death's door with meningitis, prayers were said for me in Sawley Parish Church – and that was considered remarkable. Nowadays, with seriously depleted church and chapel congregations, there is a much greater ecumenical spirit.

Music featured quite strongly in the worship at Sawley Baptist Church. Mrs Morgan played the organ (which I thought was an apt bit of rhyme) and sometimes my father pumped it, using a wooden lever at the side to give the necessary air. (Later it was connected to an electricity supply.) Singing was important both in the Sunday services and especially in the annual Sunday School Anniversary, which took place in June, one of the earliest in the season of non-conformist Sunday School Anniversaries in the area. I recall at least two years when it was so hot that the dark varnish on the crowded pews melted and stuck to clothing. It was the custom for the girls to have a new dress for that occasion, and we were all arrayed in our finery on the banked rows of platforms at the front of the Chapel, graded by size from the 'tinies' at the front to the adults at the top. I have a feeling that my father was responsible for erecting the platform, so I imagine it was builders' scaffolding supporting the hard seats. These, I'm sure, were scaffolding planks covered in cloth. We practised our anthems for weeks before the event and always sang lustily, though the music was really third rate.

Sawley Baptist Girls' Club

This was founded during the war and my mother helped to run it. She had been in many pre-war musical productions, which were popular in Long Eaton, and for one of them she had made a cat costume from black fur fabric with a hood, tail and feet. She took the tail, feet and ears off and wore it as a cosy wartime siren suit. With the Girls' Club she produced a musical play, a fairytale typical of the period, with stolen fairy princess and wicked ogre. A girl called Ivy was picked to play the ogre, much to her mother's chagrin. She came around to our house and said indignantly, "Our Ivy i'n't gonna be no ogre!", but she later relented, and Ivy played the part with gusto, wearing the 'cat' costume. Many other local women, including Miss Bennett from Bothe Hall, helped with providing materials or sewing our costumes. There were a lot of 'fairy flowers', all different, and I remember a tricky costume for a daisy where the skirt was made of lots of white fabric petals wired round the edges so that they curved outwards. I was Harebell and my dress was shot blue edged with points and I still have the little cap, made with the cut off triangles from the hem. I sang a verse of a song about *'little fairy weavers, busy elves are we'* but at the first performance some of the audience were giggling because when I stood up I was showing my pants. Mrs Morgan stepped forward and straightened my skirt.

The Sawley bomb

I recall the bomb which destroyed one of the houses which my father had built in Netherfield Road before the war. We were all in our air raid shelter when it dropped but we felt the shock and thought it must be our house that had been hit. We knew the people who were killed in the blast, Mrs Coleman and her daughter. My mother and I had that very day been with them on a trip to a church in Chilwell for a WI gathering. Afterwards we sat chatting on a wall outside Barton's bus depot and Mrs Coleman said how scared she was of air raids. We didn't go to look at the damage. The bombs were probably intended for Trent Station or the railway bridge.

D-Day preparation

It must have been in the spring of 1944 when we saw convoys of tanks being driven south along Tamworth Road. There was always some army vehicle movement in the area, because of Chilwell Ordnance Depot along the road towards Nottingham, but we all guessed this was something special. Of course, these were getting ready for D-Day. Everyone was well drilled not to make undue comments – 'Careless Talk Costs Lives' – but there was quite a bit of chuntering about the way the tanks chewed up the road surface.

Floods

I can't distinguish in my mind between the 1946 and 1947 floods and may not even have been at home for both of them because by then I was a weekly boarder at Ockbrook. The school was not affected as the Moravians built their settlements on hilltops, so it was rather more like Mount Ararat.

The floods of '46 and '47 were devastating in Sawley, particularly as it was the time of deepest post-war austerity and hardship. It must have been appalling to have spent most of the year trying to get your home dry, clean and refurnished only to have it flooded again the next winter.

Following the '46 floods the people of Canada sent food parcels via the Red Cross.

1946 Flood relief parcels from Canada

The food arrived in fairly battered cardboard boxes and was a hotch-potch of tins, many of them having been given by schoolchildren. Mrs Simpson of Draycott Lane was the senior Red Cross official in Sawley and my mother was the Red Cross Township Leader and helped to organise the distribution from the WI hall. It was a tricky job sorting the random tins into fair parcels for each of the flood victim families. The main headache with that distribution was to try to get a reasonable balance of food for each family - a good mixture of fruit, meat and veg. etc. - as it was such a medley. I can't now remember what method was used to allocate according to family size. I do remember, though, how disgusted Mother was with all the grumbles she and the other helpers had to put up with from certain recipients. They wanted more or different tins and didn't seem in the least grateful for what they had got for nothing – and off-ration.

Some of the Canadian donors had written their names and addresses on the labels and I had the job of listing them all in a notebook. A lot of tins had been collected in Toronto schools and I found one tin with the name Nancy Davies, who was my age. Mother made sure that all the named donors were sent a letter of thanks and I wrote to Nancy and kept in touch with her for nearly 40 years. She sent me several cherished presents, including my first pair of nylons.

The following year the relief food came from the Australian Red Cross and it was highly organised, not at all like the spontaneous personal gifts from Canada. Wooden crates (useful!) were packed with tinned Frankfurter sausages (delicious and highly prized), rabbit meat (much less popular) and fruit, mainly peaches, I think. There may also have been 'steamed' puddings, whether savoury or sweet I can't remember. Distribution was far easier and less controversial, but also far duller.

Flood relief from Australia 1947

Our house was never flooded but the back garden was and I remember one year when we watched the water creep up to the top step on the little flight down to the back lawn.

We also lost our beautiful shubunkin goldfish, which had come in a big tin can with perforated lid from Rickmansworth by rail. They were delivered on the LMS 3-wheeler tractor-lorry which pulled a flat-bed trailer, usually with luggage on board. The fish lived in the pond which my father made after the war, by using the bottom half of the huge 6 ft diameter Stanton pipe (3 or 4-inch reinforced concrete) which had been the core of our air-raid shelter. I remember fondly hoping the shubunkin would breed in the Trent but I doubt they got that far.

Our loss was nothing compared with those whose houses were flooded. My paternal grandparents, who lived in a bungalow in Mikado Road, were flooded both years, once with nearly 6 feet of water.

After two successive floods the flood bank was built along the Trent.

Carnivals

After the war the village decided to build a Memorial Hall and there were several schemes to raise funds, the most ambitious and potentially profitable being to resume having annual carnivals. Pre-war ones had been in aid of hospitals. A committee was formed and my father became its chairman, which took up a lot of his time and energy. I don't remember how many carnivals there were in total, but they grew both in size and popularity. For two of them the main attraction was the presence of 'Dickie' Attenborough, later Sir Richard, and then Lord Attenborough, the older brother of Sir David. Their maternal grandfather, Samuel Clegg, had been the Head of what became Long Eaton Grammar School, and Dickie was well known and loved as a film star. One year the procession was joined by a wonderful parade of antique bicycles from the Raleigh Cycle Company's collection – from hobby horse and penny-farthing through to recognisable bicycles. They were delivered beforehand to 'the workshop' in Northfield Avenue, (previously the premises of C H Reedman, Builders) for safe keeping and we had some fun trying them out.

Weather in August is always a problem and I know that insurance was taken out in case of a wash-out, but I think at least half an inch (about 13 mm) had to fall within a certain time to get a payment and there was a lot of nail-biting around the date.

The 1953 carnival was the one I was most involved in, when the committee decided to mark the Queen's coronation by having a Carnival Queen. My father was anxious that there might not be many applicants for the job and he persuaded me to enter. I was reluctant, particularly as I thought there would be talk of nepotism if I won. Three Music & Drama advisors from Derbyshire County Council Education Department came to adjudicate, and at the audition in Sawley School the candidates were handed a speech to read aloud, with five minutes to look it over beforehand. All I remember was that it included the phrase 'this high honour', which was obviously the tricky bit. I was chosen as the queen, with Sonia Smith and June Jackson as senior attendants, and Janice Mackay and Hilary Adkin as junior attendants. I had to write my own speech for the actual day, and it didn't include 'high honour'! We all were given dresses of Long Eaton lace, made to measure in Mabel Kilbourne's dressmakers' shop in Long Eaton. The attendants had dresses of Chantilly-type lace, royal blue for the seniors and white with red sashes for the little ones. Mine was a heavier white lace, and I also wore a hired red robe trimmed with white fur and 'ermine', which had been worn by a marchioness at the real coronation in June.

The almost inevitable August weather very nearly wrecked the whole day, with heavy rain throughout the morning, but enough brave souls gathered for the procession, which started in Roosevelt Avenue and the damp and shivering Fancy Dress parade contestants were duly judged. Also present were the Ilkeston Carnival Queen and her retinue, which I thought rather odd, but apparently it was their custom to attend neighbouring carnivals. Barton's buses had a special carnival vehicle which was borrowed for the procession. It was an open bus with tiers rising to the back. The little attendants sat below, and the seniors and I were on the highest level. We were led by the RAOC brass band from Chilwell and it would have been very jolly had it not been so damp and chilly. In due course we arrived at Lady Lea field on Draycott Lane and picked our way through the mud to the platform where speeches were made, and I was 'crowned' by Lady Betty Williams, formerly of Long Eaton. She was wearing sensible warm clothing, I remember.

After a tour of most of the side shows, the five of us were taken to visit several house-bound Sawley residents, including Miss Bowmer. I have a copy of *The Long Eaton Advertiser* published the following week, where the carnival report filled the front page.

I am amazed at how many things were happening at the Carnival Field that day, all reported in detail as was the custom then. Innumerable sideshows and competitions including a greasy pole and tug of war, horticultural and pet shows, a miniature railway and demonstrations involving sheep dogs, police road safety, weight-lifting, 'beating the retreat' and ballroom dancing. It all shows how much work had gone into the organisation of the event – and it was very nearly cancelled because of the weather.

Carnival Queen 1953

My Sawley life virtually ended then, because in a few weeks I left to go to college in Sussex, where I still live.

August 2018

The Tysoe's Sawley
As told to Julia Powell

<u>Margaret</u>

I have lived in Sawley all my life and I am now 83. We lived in Myrtle Avenue, New Sawley and I attended Tamworth Road School, opposite the fire station, firstly in the infants department in Clumber Street, then the senior department in St John Street. After that I went to Long Eaton Grammar School.

While the army was in our school in 1939 we were down at St John's Baptist Chapel. Eventually the men were moved to Claye's wagon works. I think it was the Derbyshire Yeomanry.

I remember my primary school teachers, Miss Dear and Miss Summers at the Infants. She taught 60 children in the hall. If you misbehaved in Mrs Hart's class, you were made to have a doll on your desk. Miss Hopkins at the Juniors dressed in strange, longish clothes. She used to sit behind her desk and pull her skirt up to put her wages up her directoire knickers, (long legs with elastic at the bottom). She used to test us every week and if we did well she gave us 3d of her own money. She pushed you on to go to grammar school and I won a scholarship. The Long Eaton Grammar School was a mixture of private and scholarship children at one time. Miss Thomson (Tomcat) was a general junior teacher.

The headmaster of Tamworth Road School was Mr Oldham (Gaffer Oldham). There was a chapel on the opposite corner to his house. The chapel is now a dental practice. His desk was at the far end of the hall, high up on a platform, and if you were naughty or late you would have to stand by the desk to be caned.

Several of us would walk through a twitchell near school, to visit a bakery at the end of Nelson Street, where we could buy fresh cream buns. One lad, John Constable, was particularly fond of these. We called him 'Cream Bun'

The headmaster of the Grammar School was Mr Roberts. We called him Dracula as that was how he looked with his dark hair and his black gown. Mr Spence, a thin man, taught English. Our maths teacher made classes real fun and we could do homework only if we wanted to, but we did. Latin was taught by Mr Crompton (Crumps), Miss Silk taught Geography and Miss Henley, Domestic Science.

I could not go outside for sport because I had a very bad skin complaint, so I had to stay indoors and complete set work. I couldn't go swimming fortunately for me but those who did found the cold water in the pool unbearable. Apparently on one occasion a boy called Brian Pearson, who later became a canon, was standing on the side of the bath with a towel wrapped around him when suddenly it was snatched away by some lads, only to reveal Brian was naked.

<u>Frank</u>

I was born in 1931 and started at Mikado Road School in 1936. There used to be Henry Smith's butcher's shop where Dalrymple's is now. They delivered meat by bicycle and they had an abattoir. When we were in school you could hear the animals squealing. I moved to Tamworth Road School in 1939 and the army were in for a period at the start of the war, beginning around September time. We started with one hour's schooling in St Mary's vestry at the little tin church on Wilsthorpe Road, then in the front room of a house situated near what was Butler's bike shop, opposite where The Royal Oak was. When we were allowed back into school we saw the wooden floors had been taken up, to enable the beds to be higher, and there were holes in the walls where the men had been playing darts.

When I was at Tamworth Road School we had to walk from school to the swimming baths from April to October. We did PE if it was too cold, but I remember one lad, who had been swimming his mile was so blue he had to be lifted out at the end. The temperature of the swimming baths could be in the 40sF (below 10degrees C) when they opened in April. The baths were built over, emptied but not filled in and still accessible, and became the Erewash Indoor Bowls Club – still there now.

Long Eaton Swimming Baths

We used to go swimming near Sawley weir. It was shallow enough to stand up in and there were little fish that you could easily catch.

During the last war I can remember standing by the shelters in the boys' playground watching aircraft in the sky in dogfights. Margaret and I can both remember the shelters in the streets being built and when they were dismantled, people rushed to collect the bricks with which they built paths and structures in their gardens.

Margaret and her parents didn't go in the shelters in the street, they slept in the 'glory hole' under the stairs on a mattress on the floor. When we were going to school if the sirens sounded, we were told if you were near home you went back, if you were near school you carried on. Guess which usually applied?

I remember a bomb dropped on two houses in Netherfield Avenue and two women in Reedman Road were killed by the blast. Also, you can still see the holes, which are now ponds, where bombs dropped at Trent Lock. Of course, the left-hand side of the golf course used to be a tipping area for railway ash and even old rail vehicles which were brought in there by train.

There were bombs dropped on large glasshouses at Shardlow. German aircraft mistook the area for Derby, where they were aiming for Rolls Royce.

One day a lorry carrying a load of tea chests hit Sawley Bridge and the tea was scattered all over the road. It wasn't too long, with rationing in force, before folks were there scooping it up! Just along where the Formula One garage is now there was a petrol filling station. On one particular day when the Home Guard was carrying out an exercise around the area, guarding the garage, a despatch rider on a motorbike arrived. As he was in 'enemy' territory he was made to carry a flag in order to fill up his tank..

Margaret and I were both in the choir at St Mary's Church, Wilsthorpe Road, as teenagers. When the anniversary took place the congregation of Sawley Church, along with the Sunday School children, walked in a procession carrying banners. The young girls wore special white dresses. Our organist and choirmaster rehearsed us to sing the traditional Hallelujah Chorus. However, he never began rehearsals until 2-3 weeks beforehand. He used to say, "You'll know this!" But you could guarantee someone would come in at the wrong time. It never happened on the night though. It never seemed to rain either. The week after the anniversary a sports event was held on Grammer's field, below the churchyard.

When we were in the choir our evening service finished before All Saints Church so we would walk from St Mary's up to Sawley Church and stand against the bakery opposite to keep warm, whilst waiting for our friends to come out of their service. There were about eight of us, including the Grammers and the Starkeys, and we'd go to a cafe along from Trent Lock for lemonades and ice creams.

As teenagers we would often visit one of the cinemas. There was The Empire, The Palace and The Scala. I liked The Palace best as they had double seats upstairs. There used to be long queues in those days and sometimes you didn't always get in. A man named Reg acted as a sort of supervisor, making sure we behaved. There was a game to get Reg over your side while the other side misbehaved.

Margaret

When I left the grammar school I went to work at Boots as a shorthand typist. Boots had a college on Station Street where they trained you and then placed you in a position in the firm. My first job was working for the manager of the penicillin works on Daleside Road, Nottingham. I was very fit then and I cycled from home every day, together with a friend who rode a racing bike. I stayed at Boots until after I was married then I left and found a new job at The Meadow Dairy in Long Eaton. That factory eventually burnt down.

Frank and I were married in April 1955 in the parish church and we had our wedding reception in the church hall (now gone) opposite The Bell in Sawley. Most of the men, not including the groom, found their way over to the pub, only to be fetched out by my Auntie Joyce.

We lived in two rooms in a big old house on Meadow Lane, Long Eaton, rented from a man called Mr Cox (Coxy). Frank had just completed his national service in the army in the February and my cousin was moving out so it was a quick job. We lived in rooms for about three years and then we had enough money to build a 3-bedroomed bungalow on a garden plot my mother owned on Owen Avenue, doing a lot of the work ourselves. It took us a year to complete. Frank travelled to work in Derby by train so when Trent Station closed in the late 1960s we moved to Harrington Street, Sawley to another 3-bedroomed bungalow which was half built and which we had altered to our liking. We lived next door to the aunt of Richard and David Attenborough. Their grandfather, Mr Clegg, had been headmaster of the Grammar School. Their mother was Mr Clegg's daughter and their father had been a pupil and a teacher at the school. In 1973 we moved to Lock Lane, Sawley, where we still live.

When my children were of school age I was instrumental in raising funds for the first swimming pool to be built at Sawley Junior School. There is so much water around here that several of us deemed it essential that children learned to swim. About ten of us parents got together and began the process. Initially Derbyshire County Council gave us a grant and thereafter we received other grants and donations and ran a football lottery. Before long we had enough money to start building so we put out tenders and Ralph Marks, a local contractor, won the bid.

We asked large firms to contribute and Hoveringham Gravel donated 100 tons of free sand and gravel. Unfortunately, on the day of delivery the foreman had gone to lunch, leaving an apprentice working in the already dug out footings. The lad allowed the truck to dump the entire load into the footings, which should have just been sand, so as not to spoil the pool liner. The load could not be dug out so another layer of sand had to be added and smoothed over again.

Both of our daughters attended Sawley Infant and Junior Schools but neither went to the Comprehensive in Long Eaton, then known as Roper School and now Long Eaton School. Jayne won the Derbyshire County scholarship which entitled her to free education at Nottingham High School for Girls until 6th form. Madeline passed the entrance examination for the High School, staying until she was 16, when she moved to High Pavement 6th Form College until she joined the RAF when she was 19. Around this time the Headmaster of Trent College was Mr Maltby and his four daughters attended the High School at the same time as Jayne and Madeline; Trent College at the time, being a boys' school.

Frank

Prior to the 1947 floods I had had pneumonia and was being attended by Dr Denny, who had a practice in High Street, where Ryley and Evans is now. He came to see me one Saturday morning and as I hadn't been out for a while he said I should get out and have a walk. Off I went with my two sisters and they decided to go to the fish and chip shop opposite the end of Myrtle Avenue. I stopped on the pavement on the other side of the road while they went across to get the fish. By the time they came out water had bubbled up out of the drains so quickly they had to walk down and jump to the middle of the road, where the camber was higher. My dad worked at Toton Sidings at the time and had to be brought home in a dustbin lorry to enable him to be dropped off through the floods.

Tamworth Road floods 1947

All round the railway bridge it was very deep and where a friend lived on Mikado Road the water had risen above the window ledges.

August 2018

John Hay-Heddle's Sawley

<u>Local businesses</u>

When we first came back to Sawley after the war the Sawley Co-op wasn't just a single shop. There was a bakery at one end, a grocery at the other, a butchery and I'm pretty sure a fish shop.

It was three or possibly four shops which weren't actually joined except by the accessways well above head height for an overhead cash railway system. This worked on suspended wires. You got your goods from the counter, the assistant tallied up the money, you handed over however much it was and possibly more if you needed change. The money and the bill went into a little container which was hooked by a bayonet fitting into the railway carriage and the assistant pulled on a handle which looked amazingly like an old-fashioned toilet handle and this pulled back the carriage on a spring load. You had to pull quite hard. Maisie, one of the little cashiers, used two hands on it. When it got all the way back it was a bit like a crossbow, it automatically released with a loud *Wang!* The little overhead carriage with your money disappeared off down the wire through the hole in the wall and you'd probably hear, depending on how close you were to the central cash desk, a clang as it arrived. You'd then have an interesting natter with your shop assistant and a couple of minutes later the thing would duly come back arriving with a clang upon which the shop assistant would undo the container, take it out and give you your receipt and any change due. The system worked but it was frantically inefficient because only one customer was served every five minutes and there was only one person manning the cash desk for the entire shop, so you might have a bit of a wait. Quite often my mother would say she'd leave it to me while she went to Billy Evans to pay the paper bill. I remember they had the sugar in pre-weighed blue bags and the flour likewise, all labelled up in ink. If you wanted currants or something you could ask for them to be weighed out for you.

Between Mikado Road and Grosvenor Avenue there was a garage, as there is now, and they used to do maintenance and sell National Benzole petrol. The pump had a diamond shaped blown glass emblem on the top depicting Mercury wearing his winged helmet. Then there was the paper shop where there's still a paper shop. It was run by Billy Evans and his wife and they had an enormous shaggy Alsatian. The shop had very peculiar smells of firewood, which was sold in bundles, dog biscuits sold in big bags along the front of the counter and tobacco, which Billy smoked in his pipe in prodigious quantities. It was quite a distinctive smell but it wasn't unpleasant.

Around 1946-47 the shop which is now Dalrymple's was a butcher's run by the Smith family. They had a nice young lad called Ken about my age. I went away to school in 1950 and when I came back at Christmas he had died of leukaemia. Next to the butcher's was H H Cox, ironmongers and where the florists is now was a chemist called Ford and Rhodes. 'Beautiful You' was a sweet shop run by the Jackson family. 'The Bakery' was Dillon's and they sold wool and knitwear patterns. It was chaos personified. I think they knew where everything was but I don't believe anyone else did! In most cases families lived above the shop in those days.

Lakeside Park was originally gifted by the Reverend Samuel Hey, for the purpose of building a school but they never used all the land. Samuel Hey was very perspicacious and according to Philip Smith, whose father used to run a barber's shop on the corner of Victoria Street, he said his grandfather remembered Samuel Hey gifting the land with a restrictive covenant to the effect that *'if the education authorities no longer need the land it shall revert to being a public open space in perpetuity for the recreation and disport of the people of Sawley'.* The Parish Council now lease the land from Derbyshire County Council.

There was always a fish and chip shop on Tamworth Road on the other side of Lakeside Park. An electrical supplier was also along there where JJL Power tools now stands. County Express used to be a beer off run by the McDermotts, a mother and daughter who rented Salisbury House up until the 1960s. They sold draught beer and people would come in with jugs to be filled. JVC Barbers was Pateman's the barber, totally appropriate because his pate was bald. Mills the florist used to sell vegetables and eggs and would deliver using a horse and cart.

The post office used to be next to the Wesleyan Chapel but had to move owing to the inability to provide disabled access. I can remember buying stamps from a machine that took pennies.

There used to be a milkman who came around with a horse and cart. He used dippers to measure out the milk into half or full pints and I still have the very jug that my mother used to receive the milk. She'd send me out with the jug and the milk would be ladled out. We had a gas fired Electrolux refrigerator then because my father needed one to store drugs. The first antibiotics, insulin and other drugs had to be kept in a refrigerator as they were deeply unstable and did not last. My parents kept the fridge until my father retired from General Practice in 1973.

John's mother's jug

Notable buildings

Shortly after the completion of the railway link between Derby and Nottingham a wealthy draper called Bradshaw decided to move out from Derby and build himself a fine mansion within a short walk from the station, which was then called 'Sawley Junction' This house, built in the mid-19th Century with a pattern of bricks of different colours on its facings, is now 192 Tamworth Road. It used to have a garden stretching all the way back to the railway line, but it has since been sub-divided.

Bradshaw and his wife had a daughter called Mary who married Samuel Clegg, who became a teacher and the founder and head of Long Eaton School – later Long Eaton Grammar School. In 1897 Bradshaw had a house built for his daughter and son-in-law to the west of his at 194 Tamworth Road called 'Rye Hill Close'. It was designed by Samuel Clegg himself in the Arts & Crafts Style. Samuel and Mary Clegg had a daughter, also called Mary, born about 1895, who in 1922 married one of Samuel Clegg's teachers, Frederick Levi Attenborough (1887-1973). For them, it is said, Samuel Clegg acquired Salisbury House, 6 Bradshaw Street, though it seems improbable they actually lived there. However, when Dilys and I returned from New Zealand in 1984 with our children and bought the house ourselves, a very old lady, Mrs. Florence Shuttler of Victoria Street, then well over 90, came around and said to us "Oh I am so glad it is you who have bought Mary Attenborough's Cottage. You will love it won't you?"

Frederick Levi Attenborough became the first Principal of University College, Leicester; later in 1957, Leicester University. He and Mary had three children, Richard an actor and director of note, later Lord Attenborough, David, later Sir David, a naturalist, conservationist and film maker and finally John, who joined the motor trade and earned a living selling Rolls Royce and Bentley motor cars to the discerning rich of Mayfair.

By the first decade of the 20th century the need for a Doctor's surgery was felt to be pressing. Accordingly, in 1908 the Clegg family had a purpose-built doctor's house and surgery built on the narrow strip of land next to their property Rye Hill Close. It was designed by architect Albert Lambert to complement Rye Hill Close in the Arts & Crafts style, complete with its Dutch Gable ends. It became 196 Tamworth Road and the home of my parents, Dr Philip and Mrs Frances (Peggy) Hay-Heddle in April 1939. Of course, war was declared in September, but father wasn't called up until two years later. At this point the senior partner gave him notice to quit. I've no idea why. While my father worked off his notice the rector took pity on him and my mum. My parents always said I was conceived at Sawley Rectory at Christmas 1941.

After war service my father bought the property from Frederick and Mary Attenborough with his War Service Gratuity. I lived there happily until I, with my wife and young children, joined the Brain Drain in 1970. Fourteen years later we returned and purchased Salisbury House, which had been sold after Mary Attenborough died in a car crash.

Dr and Mrs Hay-Heddle

I knew the Hodsons who lived at Bothe Hall. The mother had a little red MG sports car and was a prominent member of the local Conservative party. While Bothe Hall looks Georgian, in origin it is much older. What is certain is that the walls on the ground and first floors are about three feet thick. It started life as a 'fortified Manor House' in the middle ages, possibly on the site of a much earlier fortification. I am told that the remains of an encircling earthwork rampart and ditch were discovered by aerial reconnaissance at about the same time that the Church farm fortlet was discovered in the same fashion. The house was converted to its present form, with windows and doors punched through the immensely thick lower defensive walls, in the later 18th Century, once the need for defence was over.

Floods

During the 1947 floods one of the Mills family, from the boatyard on Lock Lane, was detailed to come and fetch my father every day, in a boat with an outboard motor, and take him out on his calls.

I remember we moved everything off the ground floor just in case the floods came up and in the corner there was a little inspection hatch. This was to get at the foundations and the water came up to the point where it was just lapping against the underside of the floorboards. About twenty or so years later we had, at great expense, to replace all the flooring joists because they were rotten.

Characters and pastimes

Mr Downs did door to door fish. He had a pre-war van a bit like the one in *'Dad's Army'*. Eventually he bought a more up to date Austin van. He would disappear off at dawn to go to the fish market at Grimsby to buy the fish. He'd load it into his van with lots of ice and bring it back in as fresh a condition as it was possible to be. We would buy Cod, Haddock Herring and Skate from him regularly.

We inherited a housekeeper called Mrs Dickerson when we moved into 196 Tamworth Road. She had 3 sons and her older boy Tony and younger boy Lawrence were crack shots. Also, we were friendly with another crack shot, a girl called Pippa Lawrence, Pippa and I used to go out shooting in the fields up behind Shirley Street, on Dromelow's Farm and occasionally on Grammer's land. I was about 13 and Lawrence was a couple of years older. Whoever ran Dromelow's farm at the time would supply us with .22 rifles and a full box each of 50 rounds of ammunition to go out rabbit shooting.

I got a fairground style pump action Winchester as I was quite small and we were told to go out on a summer evening and not come back until we had no ammunition left and we had cleared the land of rabbits. There were thousands and they were eating the farmer out of his livelihood. You have no idea what a plague rabbits were until the coming of myxomatosis in the mid-50s. You'd clap your hands and the whole farm would move. After the shoot we took the rabbits into the farmer who would take off the tails and skin them. Then, I suspect he sold the meat to a local butcher. For every tail he turned in to the Ministry of Agriculture he got a shotgun shell for the rifle cartridge that he'd given to us. The rifle cartridges were a penny a pop but the shotgun cartridges were a shilling each. He was making a great deal of money out of us. We didn't get paid we just got an evening's free shooting.

John, the middle Dickerson boy, didn't come out with us. He couldn't read or write but he could add up a column of figures just like that. He ended up running a building business.

For something less innocuous I used to play with the Sawley Junior Cricket Club in a field behind the Harrington Arms.

Memories of the floods in Sawley in 1947
By Shirley Syson

Many of us will remember the floods of 1947 and the havoc they caused. I was 12 years old when my home in Anstee Road became submerged in five feet six inches of dirty water. We were cut off for more than a week in March of that year. Because we had been given a prior warning of flooding we were able to move some furniture upstairs and that's where we lived for a week. There was no electricity or cooking facilities so we mainly existed on sandwiches. Bread, milk and candles were brought by rowing boat and hauled up using a rope and basket. We could see Sawley Post Office from a top window. One day we saw the two ladies who ran it open the front door, only to be drenched by the flood wave of a passing lorry. We just couldn't stop laughing. Our cat went missing during this time but was eventually found sitting on a floating lorry tyre.

After the floods went down the community spirit was marvellous. We all mucked in and helped to clean up the mess. Floors were covered in about six inches of mud so it wasn't an easy task. The Council provided disinfectant. Our house walls had a tide mark for years which kept coming through the wallpaper.

Sawley floods February 1947
Shirley's house was the small one on the right next to the end

**Sawley and Long Eaton remembered
By Jean Frearson
As told to Julia Powell.**

Sawley

I was born in my grandma's front room in Cooperative Street, off Oakleys Road Long Eaton in 1947. Across from there was the slaughterhouse and I can remember the lorries coming down. The traffic went either side of the old market place. Quite dangerous, especially later when I had my daughter in a pram.

We moved to Portland Road in Sawley and when I was five I went to the school in Wilne Road, next to where the chapel is now. I attended Sunday school at Wilne Road with lots of other kids and we practised for the annual anniversary. They erected tiers of planks for seating and the staircases each side of the chapel led to a balcony where our parents could watch. There was a path through the graveyard leading into a huge playground at the rear of Carters pop factory and we could hear the bottles rattling.

Baptist chapel and former infant school, Wilne Road

Across the road from the chapel was a farm which went through to Shirley Street. There was a row of tiny cottages which went right round into Wilne Road and that road went to Wilne before the reservoir. On Plant Lane Wright's sold posh shoes. I bought my daughter's first Clarks shoes there for £2.50. It was a fortune then. I remember there was a block of prefabricated bungalows on the lane when I was a child.

On Tamworth Road, what is now Esquina, formerly the White House restaurant, was Sawley Co-op years ago. Carters lemonade factory, now a housing complex, was next to the White Lion. Further down from Bothe Hall was a row of shops. Rooks, now a dwelling house on the corner of Tamworth and Wilne Roads, sold everything. We used to go in from school but the shopkeeper wasn't very nice. He used to throw your change at you. The shop seemed very musty and creepy.

At the top of Towle Street was the bakery and mum often used to buy me and my brother a mini Hovis loaf each. There was a chippy on Arnold Avenue but now it's a Chinese takeaway. I seem to remember there was a barber in a little house with an extension on Firs Street.

One of the buildings forming part of GT Cars on Wilne Road was my junior school where I went when I was about eight. My teachers were Mrs Bates and Miss Lorriman, she asked us to bring in oranges to eat and cut them up for us. We had school dinners in one of the classrooms. One class at the back led into a playground and there were two at the front. In 1958 there was a slight earthquake and we were sent home from school. I remember the room shook and we had to climb over central heating pipes. I didn't pass the 11 plus and went to Wilsthorpe School.

We lived in Portland Road and we often used to go down a little path through a cow field in Lock lane. The fair was always on there and when my brother was six he went on Noah's Ark and caught his leg under the ride, when he came off. It broke his leg. In the corner across from Lock Lane was a huge pond called Barker's pond.

I remember the Community Hall being built on Draycott Road. I used to go to Girl Guides there. Once we went to Hemington where I passed my test to make a phone call, pressing buttons A and B in one of the old red phone boxes. Sawley Park was just fields when I was a child and school took us on nature trips looking for butterflies. Rolls Royce and Cowburn's were up Grosvenor Avenue where there are now houses.

On Tamworth Road the post office, now a hairdresser, was the double fronted building next to the Wesleyan Chapel. On the corner of Bradshaw Street, the Dutch style house used to be a doctors' surgery.

On the other side of Tamworth Road, just beyond the railway bridge there used to be a chip shop where Formula One Garage now stands. Bains Stores was a newsagent and they had sweets in sacks and would shovel them out into bags. Dalrymple's on the corner of Mikado Road used to be a butcher's shop. Amongst the shops in that row were an ironmonger, a chemist, a wool shop and Jackson's sweet shop which is now The Bakery. I remember the Co-op, now McColls, used to weigh out the butter. They had a butchery department at one end of the shop. Next to that was Lakeside Park and the Lakeside Infants School. Beyond the park there was always a chip shop. County Express, the shop with a curved step, was the County Stores.

In the late 1950s Mills was there on Tamworth Road but it was a greengrocer. Mrs Mills would come around the streets with a horse and cart, the lights swinging on dark winter evenings while she served you. I believe she had ten children. There used to be a sweet shop next to The Bell. It's now a hairdresser. Kids went in the sweet shop when they got off the bus after school.

A community room stood where there is now a house on the corner of Charnwood Avenue. It was a tin hut with a green roof and mum used to get baby milk there for my brother who was born in 1955.

In Coronation year, 1953 we were told the Queen was going to pass through Trent Lock on the royal train. I stood with loads of others waving flags but the train whizzed past and we never saw the Queen. I was given a souvenir gold coloured model of the royal coach.

In 1967 I remember the River Trent flooded right across the fields and you couldn't see where the river was.

Long Eaton

I lived in Sawley until I got married in 1969 then we moved to Long Eaton. Shops I recall include the old post office building, set back with a wide paved area, on Tamworth Road. They had eight cashiers. After the post office was a fishmonger's and the fish was displayed on thick marble slabs. They also delivered around the streets in a van. Where RBS is now was a cheese shop, then Welch's who used to sell vegetables as well as flowers. HSBC was the Midland Bank and Rothera Sharp was a sweet shop. The Palace

Cinema was along there. If you went upstairs it was more expensive. Jay's furniture shop was where the post office is now on the corner of Regent Street. We bought a cocktail cabinet from there when we got married. The first Chinese restaurant in Long Eaton was next to Jay's. I remember dining there and when I went to the ladies toilet I had to pass the kitchen. In there I saw a huge pile of chips with a cat lying on top! TJS was a snooker hall but women weren't allowed. Later it was a Skills Shop belonging to Broxtowe College. The shop on the corner of Oxford Street was The Oxford Café at one time, before they moved over the road to Therm House. They served delicious milk shakes and coffees. Next to Barclays Bank was Keith Hall but they were upstairs then. One morning, we stood with our backs to the door of an estate agent before they opened, just along from Starkie and Gregory. We wanted to be the first inside to put a deposit down on a house because we had already lost one.

Books at The Well, formerly Anderson's, used to be Pearl's, a posh ladies wear shop. They had a big portrait of the Queen on a wall. The Oxford Café in Therm House held functions upstairs, including Christmas parties while downstairs you could choose your cooker in the Gas Showrooms. On Union Street the funeral directors was Nella Shoes. I took my daughter there for school shoes and they had lovely sandals. Kip Mc Grath was Joseph's. He trained as a hairdresser at Keith Hall. Bettys Spot Café was in The Market Place and I used to see Barton's bus conductresses in there. Max Spielman and Timpson was a double fronted shop called Wynn's which sold stockings and underskirts etc. Shoezone used to be Trueform so it is still a shoe shop. Rowells has been there ever since I can remember. Where Specsavers is now used to be a Boots shop. I recall all the little drawers and it smelt nice inside the shop. Ryley and Evans the opticians was a doctors surgery. When I had to see one of the doctors, because I had laryngitis I remember he smoked a cigarette whilst he looked at my throat. The Royal used to be a Berni Inn and when I was pregnant we went twice a week. From up the lovely staircase you could watch the steaks being cooked. There was a Plessey factory on Westgate.

I remember many of the old shops including Dewhurst's, Rose shoes, Lacey's and Gilbert's. Florence Davys on Tamworth Road sold beautiful baby and children's clothes which she kept in drawers. There were two little rocking chairs in the shop to keep kiddies amused. It is now Tobi Frames.

Memories of Carnival Day 1983.
By Jacqui Marshall

In May 1983 Sawley Infant School entered the Carnival for the first time. Meetings were organised and a committee was formed. Everyone seemed to find a hidden talent and we all got together every week to sort things out. Plessey in Beeston provided a lorry and we found a driver. We had to arrange insurance for all the people who would be on the lorry for the parade. Richard Granger and Penn Nyla kindly gave us lace and fabric for the lorry and the children's outfits. We begged and borrowed. The artificial grass used on the lorry came from a local funeral director.

There were twenty floats in the parade. Relatives and friends were volunteered for all sorts of tasks including acquiring a toilet tent and making a collapsible maypole to go under Sawley Railway Bridge. The meetings became more enjoyable as people got to know one another. Hours were spent making more than thirty outfits for children and at least twenty for adults. We trimmed umbrellas with lace for each child. We organised packed lunches for everyone and Carter's provided us with cartons of soft drinks.

When it was all over people missed the weekly meetings and couldn't wait to get started on plans for the following year.

Sawley Infants School float

Ode to the Carnival

On Carnival day we were up with the larks,
we rushed round so quickly we sure made some sparks!
Everyone had a job and they did it just right
even though some had been up half the night.
We dressed the lorry in pink and white,
flowers painted by children made it look bright.
Margaret and Jan had fingers so sore
but there they both were back for more.

Carol was there with the urn at the ready,
just filled with tea but it made us quite heady.
Suzanne was up in the cab like a pixie.
The finished result was really so ritzy.

By eleven thirty we had to be ready
with mops, caps and aprons and the toilet tent steady.
The driver arrived, said the battery was flat.
Now can you think of anything worse than that?
What would we do if it wouldn't go?
The driver said he had fixed up a tow.

Around the maypole the children sat
on artificial grass that made a soft mat.
The girls had baskets filled with flowers,
all made by Sue which had taken her hours.
Angelic boys in white shirts and frills.
Oh, please don't let us have any spills!
Streamers and banners, umbrellas trimmed with lace
and a look of joy on each little face.

The judges came around and said we'd done well.
The boys in their knickerbockers had rung the bell.
We'd made the scenery and sewed the dresses.
The girls looked sweet with flowers in their tresses.
They said they'd reward us for working so hard
and then they gave us the second award.
Three cheers for Sawley Infant School then came the cry.
I wonder how many eyes were left dry.

Along Tamworth Road we waved to the crowd.
The cheers and applause made us all so proud.
The hours we'd worked were not in vain.
I hope next year we'll be back again.

Acknowledgements for illustrations

K Reedman
Frayne chief citizen, Sawley Flood Relief parcels 1946 (2), Sawley Flood Relief parcels 1947, Carnival Queen 1953, Weight Lifting Club aerial view, Wellington Street School Breaston and Draycott Railway Station, Co-op bread van, Co-op wheelwrights shop, Long Eaton swimming baths, Mikado Road School, The Palace Cinema.

M Jennings
Grandpa and Grandma Frayne

Gary Reed
Weightlifting club membership card

Brian Reed
Market place shops and funfair Draycott

Jacqui Marshall
Carnival float Sawley

John Hay-Heddle
John's mother's jug, Dr and Mrs Hay-Heddle

Julia Powell
Mills Dockyard, Houseboats at Trent Lock today, Dr Christie memorial plaque, Baptist Chapel and former school Wilne Road, Firfield Primary School (By kind permission), Former Breaston County Primary School, Draycott Primary School, Old ads for Mrs Fearn, W H Paul, Orchard and Palm Tree Café, A Paul warmer, Jean Berrisford

Long Eaton Library
Church Lane Wilne, Mr Kind's delivery lorry 1922, Main Street Breaston.

Derby and Sandiacre Canal Society
The old canal cottages

Pat Adcock
Weights and prices from the past

Sawley & District Historical Society
Tamworth Road floods 1947

Shirley Syson
Sawley floods 1947

Karen Price
Risley Lane painting

Martin Mould
Western Mere School

Apologies are offered for any illustrations which have been inadvertently used. On notification they will be removed from the second edition.